LEARNING *from* LONDON

Church Growth in Unlikely Places

Jason A. Fout

Psalm passages are from the Psalter in *The Book of Common Prayer*, unless otherwise noted.

ISBN: 978-0-88028-478-3

Printed in the USA

Forward Movement
inspire disciples. empower evangelists.

LEARNING *from* LONDON

Church Growth in Unlikely Places

Jason A. Fout

Forward Movement
Cincinnati, Ohio

Table *of* Contents

Foreword

It is rarely a good notion to mark one's own homework. The temptation for those responsible for the leadership of any institution, including the church, is to shelter behind comforting stories that suggest things are not really as serious as the figures might suggest. Candid friends are needed to help fulfill the first duty of those in charge, which is to tell the truth about current problems and the challenges that lie ahead.

Jason Fout is just such a friend. Having heard rumors of a surprising reversal of years of decline in the Diocese of London, he decided to investigate for himself. He took the trouble to assess the evidence and talk to some of those involved in Capital Vision 2020 with its watchwords of "Confidence, Compassion, and Creativity." The results of his research are published in this book.

I was ordained in the early seventies and experienced the twenty years from 1975-95 as a time when the church in London was fearful and bewildered.

On one side of the faction-ridden leadership of the church was little more than the dull echo of the secular liberal consensus, while on the other side, there was an obstinate adherence to an anachronistic clericalist vision insufficiently rooted in Anglican tradition.

Traces of these tendencies survive. It is always a difficult task for yesterday's self-designated avant-garde to admit that they are today's busted flush.

We were an introverted church wasting our energies on liturgical fidgeting and much ado about "ministry" while elaborating a defensive bureaucracy, half a generation after other organizations had begun to simplify.

Underlying the changes discussed in this book were some fundamental pre-suppositions.

- This world cannot be understood simply as a theater of human willing. There are laws and limits, which if defied result in destruction.
- The business of life is to become attuned and aligned with the Holy Spirit.
- The task of a leader in the church is to revere the tradition but to see it as a dynamic communication between generations that must change in order to maintain the whole economy of truth.
- The leader must listen and watch expectantly for the activity of the Spirit in his or her generation, working to clear away debris and obstacles and to establish a direction of travel without being prescriptive about the details in a way that can risk overlooking opportunities.
- There must be constant reference to the way of Jesus Christ who has been revealed as the human face of God and the embodiment of God's plan for the spiritual evolution of the human race. He is the figure who is coming to meet us from the end time when the work of creation will reach its consummation.

I was consecrated as a bishop in 1992 when Francis Fukuyama's celebrated book *The End of History* was published. His thesis that the world was firmly set on a course of liberal democracy and market economics that would ultimately bring about the consummation of the human project now seems less convincing. It is time for the Christian church to recover its own eschatological vision and to confute those who believe that heaven was about twenty years ago and whose prayer is simply, "Lord, let it last my time."

The Rt. Rev. Richard Chartres
Bishop of London, 1995–2017

Chapter 1
A Growing Church: Bucking the Trend

From 1990 to 2012, the Diocese of London in the Church of England grew by around fifty percent. That the church would be growing substantially in a city that is one of the world's most diverse, multi-faith, cosmopolitan, and pluralistic is counterintuitive, to say the least. In the Episcopal Church, or more broadly among mainline Protestants in the United States, these factors are typically cited for why we need to lower our expectations and prepare for inevitable decline. In London, they are just part of the scenery.

I first heard about "something" going on in the Diocese of London back in 2009 or so. I wanted to learn more, and so when I was putting together a travel course in 2013, I included several days in London to talk with a couple of people there. What I uncovered surprised and intrigued me. I instantly wanted to learn more.

I applied for and received several grants to go back to London to spend time with folks, getting to know what was going on at ground level. I talked to people in the leafy western stretches of the city and people in the hardscrabble east; I met with people in the northern and central parts of the city; I even ventured south of the Thames to have coffee and a chat with a team of folks working in the Diocese of Southwark. I met with bishops, archdeacons, priests, pioneer ministers, lay leaders. I got to know London, its church, and its people in a much different way than I ever had. In all of these meetings, I got to hear about how these folks approach ministry in London, what they have learned, and how their churches are growing.

Since that time in 2013 and 2014 getting to know the diocese, I have led (by mid-2019) seven more travel courses, all focused sharply on the life and ministry of the Church of England in London. In those five years, about 75 people from around the world have participated: lay leaders, deacons, priests, ordinands, a bishop or two, as well as many Christians from other denominations.

Over this time, I have come to the conclusion that four key elements are contributing to the unexpected growth in the Diocese of London:

Identities and churchmanship

One of the elements I've observed on the ground in the Diocese of London is a collegial spirit across church parties.[1] There are distinctly evangelical, Anglo-Catholic, and liberal churches in the diocese. Yet I've seen much less rivalry and condescension among London Anglicans toward their siblings than I have elsewhere. I was part of a group that visited a prominent progressive church in London, and we mentioned we had just come from a well-known evangelical church. The rector spoke warmly of this other church's ministry while also differentiating it from her own church's approach. Where I expected a bit of sniffiness, there was appreciation. This is not to say that there is never any criticism or backbiting, but there seems to be more willingness to get along and even to learn from each other than I have seen in other places. This mirrors the attitude of (now retired) Bishop Richard Chartres, who was distinctly and unapologetically Anglo-Catholic in his own convictions and yet encouraged and blessed all forms of life and growth that were arising in the diocese.

Another noteworthy aspect of the Diocese of London is that it encourages distinct churchly identities. Rather than being everything for everyone and risking being nothing in particular for anyone, each church pursues its own distinct vision of its life. Each church works to be inviting and welcoming, but people are invited and welcomed into something distinct. The churches of various deaneries, when they gather, worship in the mode of the host church: evangelical, charismatic, catholic, and so forth. The diocese does not impose a "diocesan standard" when clergy or other church groups worship together, one that pretends to include all styles (and ends up disappointing them all). There is strong encouragement for churches to be who they are, and to own that identity, while also being in conversation with those who are different.

While each church tends to have a very distinct identity and to welcome people into this distinct identity, each church also has a clear sense that it is called to serve its parish—the surrounding neighborhood. (A number of "attractional" churches draw people from across the city and the region, but these are the exceptions and, through their church planting programs, are moving toward being more locally settled.) This means that the churches in the Diocese of London are focused on serving the surrounding area and its needs, not only for evangelism but in all kinds of service. This means that while a church might develop a very particular identity featuring, say, a very traditional Anglo-Catholic high mass, it does so with a clear sense of call to a very diverse local community rather than being a private club of the like-minded.

This leads to what, for many in the world, might seem a counterintuitive observation: there are blessings to establishment as it is lived out in the Church of England today. There's much more that can be said about establishment; for now, it is enough to note that part of what it means is that the Church of England is called to everybody and not just "our kind of people." While there are, without question, benefits to not being an established church, as in the United States, Kenya or Australia, it's not all gain.

Early in 2015, I attended an ordination service in the Episcopal Church during which an American bishop told me a story. He told me about a college chaplain who was leading a ministry with participation of about twelve people total, situated on a university campus with around 30,000 full-time students in residence. The bishop asked why the chaplaincy wasn't connecting with more people. One of the students piped up, saying that: "We're just not for everybody." Apparently, those involved in the chaplaincy ministry figured it ought to focus on the very few enlightened souls who already "get it." This attitude is common not only in chaplaincies but in all kinds of churches across the United States: we are too often chapels for "our kind of people."

As Episcopalians, we are too often content with—even proud of—being self-selected elites. In case this seems overdrawn, consider a cathedral congregation in one American diocese. A demographic survey of their congregation found that, among other matters, fully 92 percent of their people had a graduate or professional degree—and this in a nation where roughly 33 percent of the population has earned even a four-year bachelor's degree. I don't mean to suggest that education is anything to be ashamed of: It is certainly not. After all, I am a professor at a seminary! But this congregation, which considers itself "diverse," is anything but. Denominations in America often think of themselves as having a particular niche.

For Episcopalians, very often the niche is the educated and upper-middle class—and, in some areas, former members of other denominations. We tend to focus our efforts on these groups, "our kind of people." But this isn't the mission of Christ's church.

The Church of England, for all its foibles and imperfections, at times has a clearer sense that they are not merely a voluntary organization for "our kind of people" but are called to serve all in society in the name of Christ.

Creative evangelism

I have also noticed that evangelism in various forms is more intentionally embraced in many of the London churches, and not just the obviously evangelical ones. There is a sense that people ought to be able to talk about their faith to others, and the church needs to be able to invite people into faith. Part of this attitude may come from the reality of post-Christendom in London: the church recognizes that it can no longer take for granted that everyone knows what the Christian faith is and what Christians believe. If church members don't talk about who Jesus is and what he means, then it either won't happen at all or others will articulate the Christian faith for us, often quite poorly (think of Richard Dawkins' caricature of the faith, for example).

This need to name and explain the Christian faith has spawned programs such as the Alpha Course (and others), which are designed for people who are unchurched or de-churched to explore the faith, and be honest about questions or doubts. Beyond these explicit introductions to the faith, churches think about how they can serve the people who live, work, or otherwise move through their parish/neighborhood. The churches think not only about how to serve people but also how to *reach* them with the message of faith. Contrast this with a longstanding, widespread reluctance in the Episcopal Church to engage in evangelism (despite an explicit commitment in the baptismal covenant).

Countless stories illustrate the sad state of our approach to evangelism. Consider this real-life example: a candidate for rector of an American church asked the search committee about their evangelism efforts in that congregation. After an awkward pause, one person responded that they have an annual rummage sale, and everyone is welcome to come. Another added: "We're Episcopalians. We don't really do evangelism. We're not really interested in growing." This forthrightness might be an outlier, but I would wager it is not far from many people's experience.

I have hope that this may be changing with leadership from Presiding Bishop Michael B. Curry and other innovative programs in the American church such as Evangelism Matters, but I believe we still have much opportunity to grow when it comes to our attitudes about evangelism.

Culture of mission

Another key to understanding the church's growth in London is its culture of mission that has been instilled at both the diocesan level and in individual churches. The Diocese of London has devised several seven-year plans that articulate goals for growth and new life. They contain challenges and "big hairy audacious goals," but they also have been designed "from the ground up"—not from "top-down" directives. That is, these plans have been developed after listening to what was already taking place in congregations and building upon successful initiatives.

Another component of the culture of mission is the diocese's expectation that churches will use Mission Action Plans (MAPs). MAPs help congregations translate their vision into action, providing specific tasks with particular people accountable for and empowered to carry them out.

This culture of mission is not only found at the top though. Many churches make mission (in some form) an absolute priority. Some of these are longstanding churches, such as Holy Trinity Brompton or St. Barnabas, Woodside Park. Over the past thirty years, Holy Trinity Brompton has planted sixteen churches. St. Barnabas is committed to forming Missional Communities in its area. Other, newly planted or restarted churches are intentional about incorporating mission from the very beginning of their lives. St. Paul's, Shadwell, is one example. Restarted in 2005, the church expresses its vision as: making disciples, transforming communities, and planting churches.[2] St. Paul's takes seriously all three of these commitments to mission: Among other things, they have planted three other churches in ten years.

This culture of mission is supported and extended by a number of ecumenical Christian ministries such as London City Mission and the Centre for Theology and Community. For more than 180 years, London City Mission has worked to bring the gospel to people in the city, particularly the poor and marginalized. They provide evangelists, youth workers, prison chaplains, and community outreach workers; some of the ministries are attached to a church and some are standalone. The Centre for Theology and Community equips churches to be agents of change in their communities through the practices of community organizing, theological reflection, and prayer. Community organizing becomes a means of congregational development that benefits both the church and the broader community. The Centre also undertakes research to help churches pursue their mission. Although London City Mission and the Centre for Theology and Community are different in their missions and emphases, they both provide support for the church in London and contribute to a culture of mission.

Entrepreneurial spirit

Related to this culture of mission is an entrepreneurial spirit. But this spirit is manifested not in the sense of looking to make money or grow an empire. In fact, most clergy salaries in the Church of England are the same amount, paid from a central fund, regardless of the size of the church. This resolves much of the tension between wanting to do evangelism and concern about filling the church coffers. The entrepreneurial spirit that I have noticed in London is more a matter of being constantly alert to opportunities to serve, to meet needs, to make connections, to share the gospel, and to foster relationships with folks outside the church. One example is The Money Course, an eight-week program to help people explore their relationship with money, learning to plan, budget, and manage their finances. The course is relaxed and informal, open to anyone, and features a great deal of conversation and a bit of teaching on money and resources from the Bible. Although the designers approach the topic from a Christian perspective, it is designed to be accessible and useful to people of any faith or none. It is also possible for participants to receive help with negotiating their debts with creditors.[3]

For some, this entrepreneurial spirit compels them to not be content with business as usual. For St. Paul's, Ealing, an entrepreneurial spirit inspired them to reorient their worship space to better embody their theology, as they moved away from a traditional catholic form to a more free-flowing charismatic one. The change also made it possible for their newly configured space to be used for community functions during the week. For some congregations, the entrepreneurial spirit has led to an embrace of starkly different forms of worship: St. Luke's in the High Street decided to sell their building and move into the main shopping district in Walthamstow. They now manage the Sunday farmer's market, interact with people in the market area, and host a breakfast and Bible study.

For other congregations, this entrepreneurial spirit does not mean changing traditional forms of worship but looking for more ways that the church can serve, interact with, and invite the surrounding community. The church of St. John at Hackney cleared a large cemetery in its church grounds to allow a new green space to be used for recreation, gathering, a community garden, an open-air market, and a new play space for children in the very densely developed neighborhood. This church and its leadership saw needs in the parish and recognized that they had resources that could bless those around them. St. John at Hackney is a growing, thriving church with fairly traditional forms of worship; their entrepreneurial spirit moved them to think creatively about how to connect with the larger community.

At its core, this entrepreneurial spirit is prayerful. I have witnessed a deeply prayerful sense across styles and forms of church. I see it particularly in the way in which clergy and other leaders are alert for opportunities and are possessed of a clear sense of mission. These opportunities are not simply something else to be done, another item for the long "to do" list. Rather, they are met with a relaxed receptiveness, with a determination to discern whether this might be a chance to connect with people. In short, being alert for opportunities in this way is being alert to what God is doing right in front of us.

Intentionality and Clarity

Finally, these four elements— identities and churchmanship, creative evangelism, a culture of mission, and an entrepreneurial spirit—are tied together by two factors: intentionality and clarity.

Intentionality is crucial. These four elements have not occurred spontaneously; growth or this kind of change does not happen accidentally. Research has shown that being intentional about evangelism, church planting, and public presence are directly related to growing churches.[4] The same is true of personal spiritual maturity: it doesn't just "happen."[5] Any church wanting to grow must be intentional about it, begin to plan, and then take concrete steps. Hazy wishes in and of themselves will be fruitless, however sincere or pious.

Second, clarity is important. This means clarity of teaching and communication, but more than that, it means having a clarity of identity. Churches that are growing focus on a few things and do them well, rather than trying to be everything for everybody. Robert Warren, author of *The Healthy Churches' Handbook*, has found that churches that are growing are "focused rather than frenetic."[6] Will Leaf of St. Paul's Church, Hammersmith, expressed it as "sponsoring activity at the core." For St. Paul's, even though a large portion of the members live outside the neighborhood, the congregation focuses on the question of how they are meant to serve and love their area of Hammersmith. They have decided as a church that the staff will give particular support and prominence to ministry in the area of Hammersmith as their core mission commitment: this is their "core." They do not discourage members from other activities (indeed, they encourage them to continue them without needing sponsorship from the center), but they are clear that in the church's public activities and institutional commitments, they are called to be *in* and *for* Hammersmith.

Being clear in this way also guides decisions about which activities to pursue and which ones are outside the core mission. This does not mean that some choices are bad activities; simply that they are activities for someone else.

One final note: throughout my research into the Diocese of London, I found many sources of light and life among the clergy and churches there. As I lead courses in London exploring this growth or give presentations to clergy in America about their success, I sometimes sense from some an impatience as I discuss one or another church, as if to say, however gently or politely, “Fine, whatever, just please hurry up and get on to a kind of church that I like or agree with!” In the American church, we tend to be blithe in our dismissal and scorn those who are different from us. (As evidence, consider that the day before writing these words, a clergy colleague of mine dismissed someone else with whom he disagreed by calling him a “Neanderthal.” It matters not who the colleague or the butt of his derision was—this attitude is widespread in many forms.)

So, I must confess: I am not in the least bit interested in confirming anyone’s ideological biases. I begin, as much as possible, with no preconceived notion that one particular form of church, style of worship, shape of leadership, habit of preaching, or engagement with the sacraments, is the preferred or only possible Anglican (or Christian) way. On the contrary, I am interested in the church’s growth in all its forms: with people coming to faith in Jesus Christ; with people following him in their lives, growing in depth of faith and being involved with the sacraments; and with people struggling to understand and live that faith with full integrity in the contemporary world and working for its healing and wholeness. If there is one core conviction that informs all that follows, it is that each part of the church has much to learn from the other parts, and we are in no place to think we can determine in advance with whom we will be in conversation or from whom we may learn.

Chapter 2
Why London?

An Episcopal Church that I know, let's call it St. Swithun's, looks back fondly to its heyday. They had been led by a beloved rector for two decades. Those days saw numerical growth, a robust budget, a burgeoning facility, multiple staff people, a popular music program, a thriving ministry with children and youth, and well-attended services. Although no one would liken it to a new Pentecost, baptisms equaled funerals, and budgets were easily met. They even managed to plant a church down the road in a growing suburb. A strong wind filled their sails.

But that was decades ago. They are now in the doldrums. They have had a series of short and stormy relationships with rectors, punctuated by unfocused interim leadership. Attendance has shrunken considerably. Few children populate the five Sunday School classrooms. Adult education offerings are virtually unnoticed. A cadre of devoted older retirees populate programs offered during the week, but few if any from younger generations are similarly involved. Younger families with children often visit for a week or two, then move on. A recent annual pledge drive missed its target by 20 percent, and budget cuts loom. There is a question whether or not the church can even call a full-time rector. It seems that those attending worship do so out of a grim, dogged sense of duty rather than expectation or joy.

Does this sound familiar? For many, I imagine it does. St. Swithun's is not so unusual for the Episcopal Church in the second decade of the twenty-first century.

Those who pay attention to numbers have noticed an unmistakable trend in the Episcopal Church in the United States (and in virtually all mainline church bodies in America). Attendance and membership peaked sometime after World War II in the U.S., and both figures have steadily worn away since then. There are many reasons for this, and no doubt some loss reflects spiritual growth rather than numerical decline: Fewer people now attend church simply because it is the socially expected thing, and more of those who attend do so because of a living relationship with God and a desire to follow Jesus Christ.

And yet, from the beginning, the church has seen the source of its life in the spreading and glad reception of its message of the good news of Jesus Christ. Evangelism in all its forms is at the heart of the church's life, and although it does not always produce growth (and sometimes even brings persecution), we rightly rejoice when growth comes. And those of us who are Anglican sorts of Christians, although we are sometimes more reticent than others to be practicing evangelists, still find something of great value in sharing the Christian faith. I have met many who have come to the Episcopal Church later in life, often after leaving another expression of the faith, and have found light and life in it. They often are confused that people are not breaking down the doors to get in.

But the reality is that our doors are still firmly affixed, and fewer and fewer people are coming through them. In the most recent decade measured, from 2007-2017, Average Sunday

Attendance in the dioceses of the Episcopal Church declined by around 24 percent.[7] Membership has declined a bit more gently, shedding just over 18 percent in the same period.

Just to clarify, the two different numbers represent two different statistics. Each has some value, but both are also limited in their significance. The Episcopal Church defines membership, minimally, as having one's baptism recorded in the church. This is helpful to the extent that it quantifies who formally identifies with a given church. Yet it doesn't offer the full picture because membership rolls are often swollen with people who haven't attended or participated in the church community in years—or decades. Average Sunday Attendance (ASA) is helpful too: This statistic helps capture the number of people who come each Sunday for the primary service of worship. Just as not all members are in the pews every Sunday, not all who attend on Sunday are members. I know of a church that planned to elect a senior warden who had been worshiping with his family regularly at the church for some time and had been dedicated in his work with the church's youth. At the annual meeting where he was to become senior warden, it emerged that he had been confirmed in the Roman Catholic Church but never received into the Episcopal Church. What's more, he said that he didn't particularly want to be received and wasn't sure why it was such a big deal. Technically, according to the rules of the church, this fellow was not a "member" (and couldn't serve as senior warden), yet he was active within the congregation and committed to its ministry. The numbers, whether for membership or ASA, can sometimes be misleading.

Nevertheless, it doesn't take a math whiz to see that we can't sustain many more decades of this type of decline. We are not alone in the United States: attendance in other Anglican churches in developed nations around the world tends to mirror that of the Episcopal Church.

Some have tried to explain the decline: the Anglican tradition is said to be aesthetically and intellectually demanding and less accessible than other traditions; America is increasingly diverse, pluralistic, and multifaith; America is increasingly urban, secular, and post-Christian; fewer people are identifying themselves as Christians of any sort but are likely to describe themselves as "spiritual but not religious" or even as having no faith affiliation (ticking "none" on a survey form).

If these reasons hold any water, then it would seem that decline among Anglicans is inevitable for any similar demographic group, and this has been the case, with a notable exception: the Diocese of London, England.[8]

London could easily make a case for being the most diverse, pluralistic, multifaith, urban, secular, post-Christian environment in the West. In England generally and London particularly, fewer people identify themselves as Christian than in America, and attendance at worship services is a tiny fraction of the overall population. On a typical Sunday, only around 8 percent find themselves in any kind of church in London, whereas 36 percent of Americans attend church at least once a week, and an additional 33 percent attend regularly, if less frequently.[9]

And yet the Diocese of London has experienced marked and steady growth since the early 1990s. What factors are involved in this growth? And what forms of ministry are the churches in the Diocese of London engaged in that seem to be bearing fruit? These are the questions that animate this book.

The Diocese of London by the Numbers

From 2002 to 2012, the Episcopal Church's Average Sunday Attendance declined by 24 percent; over the same period, the

Church of England in the Diocese of London grew by 16 percent.[10] Since then, the Episcopal Church has continued to decline, with worshipers vanishing at a rate of about 2.5 percent a year.[11] In that same period, attendance in the Diocese of London held steady. As well, membership has grown, with increases in attendance among both adults and children.

Since the turn of the millennium, giving by individuals to their churches in the Diocese of London has increased by 50 percent.[12] A quick scan of numbers for the Episcopal Church over the same period shows modest growth in giving—a feat considering the numerical decline—but only rarely growing more than the annual rate of inflation.[13] In other words, despite good effort in the face of losses, giving in the Episcopal Church is failing to remain steady, owing to inflation.

One of the notable features of this growth is that it is broad-based, touching very different neighborhoods of London. There are a number of examples of striking growth. For example, St. Paul's Church, Ealing, in 1993 was home to around sixty worshipers, mostly older adults and very few children. Nine years later, average attendance grew to around 650 adults and 300 children.[14] A number of factors—which we will explore later in some depth—contributed to the growth of this church, including a change of worship style.

Or consider St. Paul's, Shadwell, in London's East End. In 2004, the church's attendance was scarcely fourteen people. After a group from Holy Trinity Brompton moved to the church to help restart it, the congregation grew to around 150 adults and fifty children on a typical Sunday. This growth has come despite the high mobility and turnover of members. Further, around 44 percent of the neighborhood is populated by Bangladeshis, a people not traditionally Christian—

although Ric Thorpe, the vicar who led the church plant, notes that a number have come to Christian faith and are now part of St. Paul's.

Or we could turn to St. Michael's, Camden Town. The church opened in the 1880s and had flourished in the past, but by the mid-1990s the congregation numbered no more than twelve. The church building and parish hall were rotting and largely derelict, without functioning toilets or heating. Although the neighborhood sang vibrantly with life, the church was thought by locals to have been closed: the only door used to access the building, a small entry in back, was unlocked for just an hour on Sundays.[15]

St. Michael's decided, with the help of a new vicar, Canon Nicholas Wheeler, to open their front doors as often as possible so that people could come in off the streets and to open their gates so folks could sit in the garden (a green space that was a luxury in the neighborhood). They determined to make the church available to the surrounding community, hosting meetings and concerts. A newly built supermarket, which is said to attract around 55,000 shoppers a week, opened near the church, greatly increasing the foot traffic. The congregants have grown to be much more open and welcoming to newcomers rather than trying to hold on to a hidden private chapel. While attendance has grown to around 100 on Sundays, closer to 300 people see St. Michael's as their church, with their connection to its many weekly services and other ministries. (This is despite a heating system they describe as "woefully inadequate"!)[16]

There's also St. Ann's, in Tottenham. This area has the highest unemployment rate in London and one of the highest rates of poverty in the United Kingdom. The area around the church is known as the most ethnically diverse in all of Europe, with around 300 languages spoken. Tottenham has known its share of civil strife, in part from the relationship between (largely black) residents and the area's (largely white) police force. In 1985, residents rioted on the Broadwater Farm Estate in response to the death of Cynthia Jarrett, who suffered heart failure during a police search of her home. In August 2011, Tottenham resident Mark Duggan was shot and killed by a police officer. Two days after his death, a peaceful protest march was followed by five days of looting and arson. These 2011 riots began about 800 yards from the front door of St. Ann's Church.

When John Wood arrived at St. Ann's to serve as vicar in 1994, attendance hovered around ninety people. This doubled in the first year, even though John suffered from clinical depression and neither preached nor led worship services during this time. By 2010, average Sunday attendance had grown to 410. Over this time, the budget of St. Ann's (including social action projects) increased from £30,000 to over £600,000, the staff grew to forty people, the buildings were comprehensively rehabilitated and fully used, and they started five new congregations.[17]

These stories are the tip of the iceberg. There are many more stories of less dramatic but no less real growth as well. Later in the book we will turn to closer consideration of some of the factors behind this growth; for now, it is enough to highlight some of the more dramatic turnarounds.

Explaining London's Church Growth

So, is the Diocese of London's growth simply an illusion? Some say so.

When they hear of the surprising growth in the Diocese of London, many people have a quick and simple explanation.

One colleague of mine wrote it off, insisting that it was entirely explained by immigration from African nations such as Nigeria. My colleague's insistence on a single, simple, and largely dismissive explanation for the growth is common. The diocese itself admits (and pushes back against) this tendency of what they call "knockdown arguments," an "instant, single, knockdown reason why it may be happening" in London, with the implication that it could not happen elsewhere.[18] Here are some of the most popular "knockdown arguments" that dismiss London's growth as an aberration:

1. "The population is growing in London faster than elsewhere, and so the church is 'growing' by riding a rising demographic tide."

2. "There is more immigration from abroad in London than elsewhere, and immigrants are more likely to attend church than native British folks."

3. "London claims an outsized share of talented clergy, and so naturally that diocese is growing, being well-served by the brightest and best."

4. "London is populated with lonely people looking to make connections with others, and church is one place to do so—but this doesn't mean the churches are populated with dedicated Christians."[19]

5. "The growth in the Diocese of London is fueled by the churches associated with Holy Trinity Brompton (HTB) and its program of church planting. Take them out, and the numbers will look different."

The Diocese of London admits that there is a kernel of truth to each of these points, but they do not in themselves explain the substantial growth of the church there. For instance, it's true that the population of the city of London has exploded over the last two decades. Clearly this contributes to the diocese's growth. However, this population theory does not explain why the Diocese of London has seen significant growth over the last two decades while the dioceses of Southwark and Chelmsford, which also include large sections of the city of London, have not.[20] At the same time, folks in the Diocese of London also point out that their growth figures are not actually keeping up with the growth rate of the population as a whole.

The fact is that membership and attendance numbers in the Diocese of London show a clear downward trend through the 1970s and 1980s. The city's overall population was already increasing in the 1980s, but it was only in 1990 and beyond that the church in the Diocese of London began showing sustained and steady growth. Finally, it is clear that demographic growth does not necessarily translate into church growth elsewhere in the world, so why should we assume it to be so in London?

Take, for example, the Episcopal Church in the United States. At General Convention 2000, the church adopted a resolution entitled "20/20: A Clear Vision" that proposed to double the size of the church by the year 2020. Proponents presented this as a "big hairy audacious goal"—a BHAG—using the phrase introduced by Jim Collins and Jerry Porras. Through the first seventeen years of this program, according to the US Census, the population of America has grown by about 43 million, or roughly 15 percent. Yet the Episcopal Church's numbers, as we saw at the start of this chapter, show that far from gaining from this population growth, the church has continued to hemorrhage members.

As to the second point, immigration—both from within and outside the European Union—has indeed been an increasing feature of London demographics. Yet, for all the growth, the percentage of Christians in London is shrinking, while groups such as Muslims or "nones" are growing quickly. Certainly, some immigrants from various African nations are amenable to the Anglican expression of Christianity—and this influx represents real and significant growth, not to be written off. But many more African immigrants attend independent, black-majority churches in London, and Christian immigrants from the EU tend to come from countries such as Poland that are historically Roman Catholic or Eastern Orthodox. Looked at another way, rather than being a demographic wave destined to lift the Church of England's membership, immigration might be seen as a means through which the church could simply be left behind as a relic of another time.

It is true that talented clergy in the Church of England are very often attracted to the southeast of England, including London, and vacancies fill much faster in this part of the nation than in other areas.[21] However, some churches in London have trouble attracting clergy as well. Some priests with children are deterred by the reputation of many of the local schools in the city. What's more, many of the clergy leading the growth in London were raised up within the diocese rather than attracted away from elsewhere—and London sends many clergy out to the wider church as well.

It's true that many young adults come to the city of London to make their way in their careers and are looking for social outlets and connections. However, this is nothing new and does not explain the diocese's uptick since 1990. Certainly young adults across the UK and around the world manage to find social outlets without turning to the church.

Holy Trinity Brompton (or HTB) has, since 1985, planted sixteen new congregations in and beyond London, and has been indirectly connected to a further seven congregations.[22] HTB and its church planting program *have* contributed significantly to the growth in the diocese. In the seven years leading up to 2010, 38 percent of the growth in Usual Sunday Attendance (equivalent to Average Sunday Attendance) in the diocese came from churches associated with planting programs at Holy Trinity Brompton and St. Helen's Bishopsgate (another large evangelical congregation).[23] But this commitment to church planting isn't the sole purview of two congregations. Church plants and restarts are now coming from a range of churches with a variety of models. These include St. Ann's, Tottenham, which we discussed earlier, as well as many others that are undertaking modest and inexpensive startups, even within their own present facility. Church plants of all sorts are contributing to the growth of the diocese.

Each of these points describes relevant features of the context of the Diocese of London, but none provides a comprehensive explanation for its growth. Demographic changes alone do not explain the church's revitalization in the Diocese of London. Clearly, the diocese's success is not simply a matter of making sure the church's doors are unlocked so that the newcomers might stream in.

Indeed, it might be easy to read this book and think, "it must be easy in London." The stories I tell here are mostly stories of churches that are doing creative ministry and churches that are growing. But it is important to keep this in context. First, there has been substantial growth in the Diocese of London since the early 1990s. But the numbers seem to have flattened out since 2015. It's not clear what, if anything, this might reflect, at least not yet. Often the significance of such things only becomes clear in hindsight.

Plus, across the diocese, the growth is focused in about thirty percent of the churches. Roughly 20 percent are maintaining steady membership. This leaves around 50 percent that are experiencing decline. Although the numbers overall show some health, this is not universally the case as though a rising tide were raising all the boats. The research of the Centre for Theology and Community has shown convincingly that growing churches plan for growth, approach it intentionally, and have leaders who are dedicated to it. Growth does not happen inadvertently.

This growth is also more often found in larger churches than smaller churches. Although the one church, one vicar model is important to London—rather than sprawling team ministries or part-time vicars, often found in other parts of the Church of England—evidence suggests that it is also important to have a congregation that is invested in the vision of the church and its ministry in the parish. One priest, no matter how competent, faithful, and dedicated, cannot do the work of the entire church. Many thriving churches complement the ministry of a vicar with a team of laypeople—some volunteer and some as part- or full-time employees.

The growth has not been effortless but has come through the hard work of evangelism, community service, team-building, and meeting people where they are found—which in one form or another have been the church's tasks from the beginning. It is to that work we now turn.

Chapter 3
Lead. Or Get Out of the Way.
How the Diocese of London Supports and Encourages Mission

During a presidential election season in America, a common narrative is that not only is Washington in its present form "broken" but also that nearly any large-scale governance is apt to be dysfunctional. Leaders are "out of touch"—isolated, distant, self-protective. Politicians don't understand life "on the ground." Any genuine innovation or adaptive change will come at the local and individual level, rather than the national.

It doesn't take much searching to find this same language used in various dioceses of the church, whether by clergy or lay leaders. They bemoan bishops and diocesan staffs as "under-functioning" and "out of touch," isolated and self-protective. If this is true of the diocese, how much more is it true of "815," the shorthand moniker of the headquarters of the Episcopal Church (located at 815 Second Avenue, in New York)? The usual prescription for both government and church is for the person or organization to simply get out of the way.

Yet, the Diocese of London shows us that this is not the solution. In fact, substantive change and growth in the diocese have been embraced and promoted both by the leaders at the top and by clergy and people at street level. In this chapter, we'll look at how the diocese has encouraged and incentivized health and growth from the center. Later chapters will look at this health and growth from the perspective of congregations and other ministries.

Encouraging Growth with Parish Share

In London, the diocese has become intentional about using administration to facilitate growth. To understand this, we need to take a brief look at how the Church of England divides the whole of the nation into parishes. These parishes are geographic and demographic: They are about the entire population living in an area. As it is often said, every blade of grass in England grows in a Church of England parish. A priest is therefore the vicar of a *parish*—the entire group of people in an area—and not a chaplain to a church. This understanding of parish creates an expectation that the vicar is a presence in the community (the parish)—and not only to perform baptisms, marriages, and burials ("hatch, match, and dispatch," as it is jokingly called). The priest is often expected to provide some religious education teaching in local schools and to be engaged with youth clubs, civic society, and local community. The vicar is to be present to all, not merely members of the Church of England but also to Methodists and Muslims, atheists and the unengaged. In the English context, the parish is communal (about a community) rather than associational (about a self-selected group). This is different than in America, where we most often use the word "parish" to mean "church."

Another important difference is the source of compensation for clergy. In the Episcopal Church, congregations call their own clergy, with varying degrees of input from the diocese. Mission congregations have the most diocesan involvement: They are dependent upon financial assistance from the diocese, and in most cases, the bishop is considered the rector of the congregation with a vicar serving locally. Whether parish or mission, congregations within the Episcopal Church pay the salary for clergy. This can create quite a disparity, with some affluent churches able to compensate at a higher rate and call multiple full-time staff. Other churches may only be able to call one priest at a lower salary or even only part-time. Some churches can only afford supply—that is, paying a priest a small stipend for leading Sunday services.

The system in the Church of England is very different. In England, the church operates a "parish share" system in which each parish pays its share to a common fund in the diocese—the wealthier and larger pay more, while the poorer or smaller pay less. This money is then used by the diocese to pay the salaries and benefits for clergy. The individual churches of a diocese work together to provide pastoral care across the entire diocese. The "parish share" is calculated in various ways but the amount requested is based generally on church membership. This allows for churches in sparsely populated rural areas and down-at-the-heel urban parishes to be served by clergy in the same capacity as churches in a thriving city center or suburb. There is a fairly clear sense, at least ideally, that the churches are all in it together, rather than each being on its own.

This approach allows for churches to be staffed by clergy in rather poor neighborhoods. For example, take St. Nicholas, Poplar, which is located on the Aberfeldy Estate in the East End of London, an area with higher joblessness than elsewhere in the capital. The church is a part of the larger parish of All Saints, Poplar. As we will hear about more in chapter seven, St. Nicholas was reopened in 1998 after being closed for nearly thirty years, in order to serve the people in the area. Under the leadership of clergy such as Jane Hodges, the church has seen marked and steady growth. This sort of work, in a depressed area that might not itself be able to support a church building or clergy person, is made possible by the parish share system.

Of course, the parish share approach has the potential to provide *disincentive* for growth. If larger churches are expected to pay more while smaller churches pay less, some might be tempted to underreport numbers or make strategic decisions against growth that might cost more money. The parish share approach might even seem like a subsidy to underfunctioning churches. The Diocese of London anticipated these concerns and addressed them. Until 1994, a parish's giving to the Common Fund was determined by a formula that included the size of the church. The next year, giving was changed from a fixed formula to "a system of bids and agreements within deaneries."[24] This allowed churches to make a case that they might make a lower contribution for a certain amount of time so that the funds could be used for mission and growth in their own parish.

For example, St. Paul's, Hammersmith received a "transplant team" in 2000—a group of people from a nearby congregation who moved to St. Paul's to implement a strategic plan for growth and development. The church was given a three-year grace period, during which they paid only a fraction of their typical contribution. This allowed the people of St. Paul's to use their financial resources to support their growth directly. In situations of planting or substantial new growth, this approach can be particularly important, as giving lags behind attendance. New members often attend for a while before becoming givers.

While the parish share system has both positive and negative aspects (as do other "self-funded" churches across the Anglican Communion), the possibility of a "grace period" is an important example of how the Diocese of London has acted proactively to encourage growth.[25]

Creating Mission Action Plans (MAPs)

Another way the diocese encourages mission and growth is an expectation for all churches to develop Mission Action Plans (MAPs), documents that express the values and goals of each congregation. Each parish is responsible for putting together its own MAP; the diocese does not decree their shape or priorities. The MAPs are intended to be highly contextual and particular to each church and parish. They change with the needs of the parish, the size of the church, the church's self-conception, and so forth. The diocese recommends that the task of creating the MAP should involve as many people as possible from across the congregation.

Shortly after Rob Wickham arrived as rector of St. John at Hackney, he began a year of listening. This was intended to be a process of fact-finding and considering what St. John's was *for*. He formed three groups with particular tasks. The first was dedicated to the question, "What is Hackney?" This question prompted a close look at the surrounding neighborhood and the people who make it their home. The second group asked the question, "What is this building—the church—and what is it for?" The final group looked at questions of sustainability, particularly in relation to the churchyard, which had recently been restored to be a green space for the neighborhood but needed more intentional care. Each of these three groups involved about ten members of the congregation, with Rob as the convener. People from the surrounding area were also invited to speak to the groups as a form of community input and audit.

After that first year, each of the three groups came back with a series of proposals for the next five years. The church took a month to pray about the recommendations. And then over a weekend, the proposals and feedback from the congregation were incorporated into St. John's MAP, a five-year plan called

The St. John at Hackney Project. This focused on three primary goals:

1) To restore aspects of the building to help tell the story of God's work in Hackney, which included a reordering of the worship space;

2) To open up the building more, especially to the community, local businesses, and creative industries; and

3) To be more intentional about ministry with three particular groups: children and young people; elders; and those needing help with their health.[26]

The goals set in this project were completed by 2012, and in 2013 the congregation celebrated the conclusion of this five-year MAP and entered into a new one, called Oasis Vision 2018, which had come about through a similar process of listening and consultation.

For their mission, they articulated their call to be:

1) A spiritual hub, walking with Jesus, from the heart of Hackney to its margins;

2) A place of worship, haven, and sanctuary open 24 hours a day; and

3) An oasis in the wilderness.

And as part of moving ahead in this mission, they set themselves the objectives of:

A) Developing new leaders who reflect our diversity; and

B) Opening the building for prayer and sanctuary 24 hours a day.

Further, they sensed a call to focus their mission particularly on those living in isolation, on 20- to 35-year olds, and on children and young people.[27]

The work at St. John, Hackney, is just one example of a MAP. The diocese intends MAPs to be attentive to particular congregations and contexts rather than a cookie-cutter process. Their value lies in giving congregations an opportunity to reflect on their history and to be honest about their strengths and weaknesses as well as to think intentionally about the future. It also gives church members a chance to set some SMART goals (objectives that are "Specific and Stretching, Measurable, Achievable, Relevant and Realistic, as well as Time Bound and Timely"[28]). Congregations are challenged to think about mission in particular and concrete ways rather than in general platitudes. These goals are then established as short-, medium-, or long-term. The process, as at St. John's, is meant to be collaborative, so that the whole congregation has buy-in to the plan. As the MAP comes together, churches launch their new vision with a celebration, which includes involving members of the broader community. Over the life of the project, the individual goals on the MAP are monitored and assessed so it does not simply get lost behind a file cabinet somewhere as one more well-intentioned but unexecuted enterprise. St. John's provides an annual magazine-format update (in a downloadable PDF) to document the progress on the MAP.

The Diocese of London has held out MAPs as a "best practice" for churches to live their mission intentionally. The diocese has not done this by demand or fiat but rather through a clear expectation that churches devise and put a MAP into place—and the diocese provides resources to support the process. In this way, the diocese encourages a culture of mission, with each church individually taking initiative and responsibility for its own vision and ministry.

Envisioning mission in the diocese

The Diocese of London has also set out a number of vision statements for its own life. From 2002 to 2012, the diocese set out the London Challenge as a strategic framework for its mission. This was intended as something of a diocesan MAP.

Crucially, the London Challenge was not meant as *something else* for busy congregations to adopt. In fact, the diocese worked to reduce the diocesan-level demands made of congregations. For example, Richard Chartres, when he was made Bishop of London, decided early on to pare down the governing and consulting bodies in the diocese, which he considered "black hole[s] of energy." At that time, lay and clergy leaders served on committees for unity, mission, ministry, social responsibility, and many other areas. The committees had begun with the aim of increasing participation in the diocese; however, the effect was a draining of energy. So much time was spent in rounds of meetings and consultations that little energy and time was left to actually engage mission. As Bishop Chartres puts it, "No one has ever said to me 'if only we had a Board of Mission we would have done some mission.' "[29] The focus moved to the churches and how the diocese could assist in their work of mission and ministry.

In developing the diocesan vision statements, the catchphrase was "add up, not add on." These were not to be another set of top-down mandates to be added to the busy-ness of parish life but an opportunity to take stock of all the ways the church was already living out its mission. This meant that rather than being passed down from on high, the vision for the diocese was intended to "trickle up" from street level.

To draw all of this together at the diocesan level was a way of highlighting the good work happening in the parishes as well as concentrating and deepening the diocese-wide commitment to these tasks. The London Challenge included seven commitments:

1) We are committed to sharing the good news of Jesus Christ in twenty-first century London;

2) We are committed to equipping the servants of Jesus Christ;

3) We are committed to telling the story of Jesus Christ afresh for this generation and especially for the young;

4) We are committed to serving London and all her people;

5) We are committed to expressing God's love in our World City;

6) We are committed to making four Capital Investments[30]; and

7) We are committed to generating the resources in finance and property to enable the church to respond adequately to the London Challenge.[31]

These commitments reflected the best work already going on in the diocese and also held this work up as a communal challenge to continue growing in this way. Each of these commitments makes explicit and intentional the church's life of mission. Each of them turns the church's attention beyond itself and well beyond maintaining a building or institution for its own sake.

The successor to the Capital Challenge is Capital Vision 2020. It was in development for some time and formally inaugurated in the summer of 2013. As with Capital Challenge, Capital Vision 2020 collects together what the church is already doing well at the grassroots level in order to make intentional commitments in these areas. As before, the tagline is still "add up, not add on."

The diocese's approach in developing the Capital Vision 2020 was to be open and consultative, engaging as many churches as possible. In March 2012, the Bishop of London asked every church to discuss the following three questions:

- What is the Holy Spirit saying to us in the life of London?
- Where do we focus effort and resources?
- In what ways do we need to rethink and act differently?[32]

Some two thousand people were involved in the discussions that led to Capital Vision 2020, meeting in churches, as part of specially convened groups, and participating in an online survey. The responses were brought together and discussed by a working group of diverse professionals, who identified three particular themes that arose consistently. These three themes and their objectives share a vision of a church that is Christ-centered and outward looking:

1) We seek to be more confident in speaking and living the Gospel of Jesus Christ. To enable this we will by 2020:

    a) Communicate the gospel more effectively, using the opportunities offered by new media;

    b) Equip and commission 100,000 ambassadors representing Jesus Christ in everyday life; and

    c) Invest in leadership and increase the number of ordinands by 50 percent.

2) We seek to be more compassionate in serving communities with the love of God the Father. To enable this we will by 2020:

a) Enable new initiatives to fight poverty, inequality, and injustice in London and worldwide, including our joint venture with the Church Urban Fund.

b) Open up our church buildings to the wider community.

c) Strengthen links between schools and their local Christian community.

3) We seek to be more creative in reaching new people and places in the power of the Spirit. To enable this we will by 2020:

a) Double the number of young people involved in local Christian community.

b) Create or renew 100 worshiping communities.

c) Engage more closely with sports and the creative arts.

d) Each pray for at least seven people that we may share with them the story of our faith.[33]

I earlier briefly mentioned Big Hairy Audacious Goals (or BHAGs).[34] The London diocesan objectives might not technically be BHAGs, but they were certainly audacious. For example, the diocese committed itself to commissioning 100,000 "ambassadors representing Jesus Christ in everyday life": this is particularly audacious when you consider that the baptized membership of the entire diocese is only around 72,000 people.[35] They spell out being an "ambassador" as a form of "whole life discipleship." The program provides education and encouragement for baptized Christians to live their faith in the world.[36] However they might achieve it, this goal will require more people than they have on the rolls presently, whether through growth or connecting ecumenically with other Christians. They are not content with the status quo.

In 2018, six years into the Capital Vision initiative, the diocese reported they have commissioned nearly 40,000 people as ambassadors. While it seems likely they will not meet their goal of 100,000 by 2020, the bold stretch goal inspired the diocese to create and distribute resources to empower and encourage 40,000 people in their faith—and those 40,000 in turn have touched innumerable others. As the diocese prepares for the next vision statement, they can return to this goal, evaluate whether it was worth doing and ask what they have learned and how they might continue to improve.

Or to look at another BHAG, consider the commitment to "create or renew 100 worshiping communities" by 2020. This sounds substantial but its audacity becomes even clearer when you realize there are only eighty-four months in seven years: this commitment involves creating or renewing more than one worshiping community a month. Again, the diocese (intentionally) left this objective flexible. Although a good number will be new church plants, church transplants, and restarts, the goal is "worshiping communities." Some will involve launching of new congregations through starting a distinct service at an existing church or establishing regular gatherings for worship that may not appear like a traditional parish church. For example, some congregations, known as "network churches," meet at rented facilities near transport nodes such as railway stations where it is easy for people spread throughout the city to gather. In fact, one such church is called KXC, for King's Cross Church, which meets near King's Cross Station. Some others of these will be Fresh Expressions of Church, Missional Communities, or Pioneer Ministries, which I talk about more later, in chapter eight.

This flexibility in implementation is important. Different groups in the church accomplish these objectives in their own particular ways: an evangelical, a catholic, and a progressive broad church might work toward the same goal ("communicating the gospel more effectively") but undertake it in rather different forms.

While these objectives are both audacious and flexible, they also manage (by and large) to be SMART, as explained above. They are stated concretely enough that one would know whether or not they have been achieved. For example, if the number of ordinands only increase by 30 percent in the allotted seven years, that goal will not be reached. Or if fewer young people are involved in local Christian community than when the initiative began, the diocese will clearly have not achieved its objective to double such involvement. If, in 2020, more church buildings are open to the local community—whether for midday prayer, AA meetings, charitable groups, or social space such as a café or a money advice clinic—then the diocese can say that it has reached the objective.

More can be said about how the diocese has worked to encourage an ecology of mission, but I'll finish with this story. Bishop Chartres was himself strongly and unapologetically catholic in his Anglican identity. But he was very clear throughout his episcopacy that, as he puts it, "every legitimate strand in the Anglican tradition should be honored and reflected in the appointments made in the diocese. There is only one vital distinction which transcends the differences between different strands of churchmanship and that is the distinction between dead church and living church."[37] He blessed and supported life and growth in the diocese in all sorts of forms, from traditional catholic to charismatic evangelical to liberal catholic to broad church. This has in turn contributed to a spirit of openness and appreciation among the different groups that is not often found in the church in America. To put it another way, this way of approaching the matter means that the main concern is not ensuring that my church party wins while yours loses but rather focuses all of us on Christ's mission in the world.

Chapter 4
Following the Spirit: Holy Trinity Brompton

Some time ago I was visiting London over All Saints' weekend and thought I might try out a new church on Sunday. Looking at my options, I chose Holy Trinity Brompton. I had heard some of the buzz of the church's growth, and I could wander around Knightsbridge after church, killing some time before an appointment in the afternoon. The later service time that morning was 11:30, which I thought would make a nice start to the day. I planned out my trip to the church so that I could arrive ten minutes early. Although I love church buildings, I happen to be partially deaf, and some churches can be great echoing barns, making it hard to hear. So I like to come early to a new church so I can sit somewhere I can hear.

I came up out of the tube station to the weak sunlight of an English autumn day and walked to the church. As I approached, I gradually noticed more and more people heading in the same direction. I wondered what was going on. Coming to the church itself, I realized that most were headed to the same destination. As several people greeted me, I proceeded up the steps into a repurposed Gothic space whose rafters thrummed with the roar of a church that teemed with worshipers. People sipped coffee, visited with each other, welcomed newcomers, and found a place to sit.

Arriving there almost felt like a sensory overload. When I collected myself, I realized my plan to arrive early for the best seat had been thwarted: The place was packed. I found my way into the balcony, where I managed to snag a chair at the farthest back point on some risers. Very nearly every other seat had been spoken for, and shortly after it was standing room only.

The service lasted about an hour. Rock-pop oriented music drove the worship, with the praise band on a stage in front, with drums and guitars. Announcements were made through a professionally crafted video presentation on TV screens. The sermon lasted about a half hour, with some slides included, and focused on making scripture applicable to life. There was no formal liturgy, no prayer books, no vestments, no communion, no liturgical reading of the Bible. Only after lunch did I remember it was the Sunday after the feast of All Saints, because it hadn't been mentioned in church.

Reflecting on this visit, I noticed three things. First, the congregation was incredibly diverse; I'm tempted to say it was made up of people "from every nation, from all tribes and people and languages" (Revelation 7:9). People of vastly different racial and ethnic backgrounds worshiped alongside each other naturally and joyfully. The band on stage reflected this as well. I did not stop to ask anyone where they were from, but I caught snatches of non-native voices alongside the usual jaunty jumble of British accents. People attended alone or with their families or with friends. I could not recall ever having worshiped among such racial and ethnic diversity before. Most of us in America have become inured to worshiping during what Martin Luther King Jr. called "the most segregated hour of the week."

Second, the service was characterized by an energy the likes of which I had not experienced in worship for some time. People sang with enthusiasm; some raised their hands or swayed. The music pulsed with energy. The songs spoke in a range of voices, from praise of God to repentance and renewal, to being committed to acting for a better world. Lyrics were shown on screens around the interior of the church. As we all sang together, I felt a powerful sense of being all together in one place, praising God. To put it bluntly, people seemed excited to be there. This may contrast with the experience of some, for whom "being excited to be in church on Sunday" might seem like a category error.

And finally, I was struck by how young the people present were. Some were middle age, and I recall a few older folks, but unlike many churches, they were not the majority. There were some established families: I sat among one extended family who spoke with Anglo-African accents. There were some younger families as well, but the largest group by far were people in their twenties who appeared to be without children and likely without a mate. Here, in London, reputed to be one of the most post-Christian cities in the West, was a church overflowing with Millennials, alleged to be one of the most post-Christian generations in the West. In case it was a fluke, several months later I returned, visiting a late afternoon service, and it seemed to be filled with even more folks in their twenties. It was, for me, a disorienting experience: Being in my mid-forties, I have become accustomed to bringing the average age *down* in any given gathering of Episcopalians. (While in seminary, at my field education parish, my wife and I were at least fifteen years younger than the youngest adults and roughly fifteen years older than the oldest children.) At Holy Trinity, to my dismay, I began to feel my age! But it serves to highlight the contrast with the usual church, where the Millennials seem to be a "lost generation."

How did Holy Trinity Brompton—or, as they're often known, "HTB"—get here?

+ + +

The main location of HTB sits in the posh South Kensington district of London, a stone's throw from the Victoria & Albert Museum and a quick walk from the famous department store, Harrod's. The church building itself sits behind a Roman Catholic church, down a leafy passage off of the Brompton Road, and appears unremarkable. It might be easy to miss.

But the impact of HTB and the Alpha Course (which began at HTB) are unmissable. Around 4,500 people worship here every week. At any given time when an Alpha Course is running, around 1,500 are involved in the program, investigating the Christian message. Through its approach to leadership, its efforts in church planting, its pushing the envelope on Anglican worship forms, its emphasis on practical teaching, and its unapologetic appeal to young people, HTB has left a lasting mark on the Diocese of London and its life.

Renewed by the Spirit

The church of Holy Trinity Brompton has been in existence since the 1830s, founded by another church, St. Mary Abbott. It was, into the 1970s, a fairly traditional, staid evangelical Church of England congregation. In 1976, Sandy Millar became curate and was given responsibility for the Sunday evening service. He began, very slowly, introducing guitars into the worship, alongside traditional hymns. This service began drawing in young people. In many ways, these young people, their strong faith, and their determination to live it out, became the fuel for the engine of the growth of this service and HTB generally.

In 1980, John Collins became the vicar of HTB. John had been touched by charismatic renewal, a multi-denominational movement that emphasizes the presence and activity of the Holy Spirit, seen in vibrant worship, charismatic gifts such as being given a word of prophecy, and prayers for healing. The church at first wasn't sure how to respond to John's approach. A visit in the early 1980s by John Wimber, the American evangelist and leader in the charismatic Vineyard Movement, was a turning point.

John Collins had extended an invitation to Wimber to come and visit and do some teaching for the leadership of the church. Wimber came in the morning and spoke about healing. At one point there was a break, and Wimber said, "Now we're going to have some coffee, and when we're done we're going to do some healing." Mark Elsdon-Dew, a lay leader on the church's staff, was there. He reports that the group had no idea what Wimber was talking about—but "it was the longest coffee break ever!"

When the church leadership finally came back together after the coffee break, Wimber spoke some words of knowledge—messages that, in prayer, he sensed that God had given him to speak. One of the messages was that there was a woman there who was trying for a baby but was barren. Sandy, the curate at the time, says that "we were all very cultured people—many of the people had jobs in the city, we were sophisticated. We were all very polite to one another. We loved one another. But we never talked about these things—this was a very personal thing that we in our British way would never talk about. Nevertheless, I knew all of these people in the room, and I *knew* that none of them fell into that category.

"And then, to my surprise, this young woman came down to the front and said, 'that's me.' We were all staggered."[38]

If they were stunned by the revelation, they were even more shocked by the outcome. Wimber prayed for her—prayed with boldness that she would be healed. And nine months later, the woman gave birth to a baby. Others also experienced healing during the session. The staff had never seen the likes of this before, but it brought a decisive shift to the culture of the church.

Partly this shift has been an openness to what are known by some as charismatic gifts: healing, words of knowledge, words of prophecy, and so forth. That said, in the times I have worshiped at HTB, these elements have not usually been front and center. There is often a time after the close of a service where worshipers can come forward for prayer, and this might be introduced by a message such as, "You're welcome to come forward for prayer, for anything. But we have a particular sense today that there might be someone here needing prayer for X. If that's you, please come forward; we'd love to pray for you today." Such prayer is, in my experience, warm and extemporaneous but not hugely demonstrative. Often, someone praying for you might share a word of knowledge, encouragement, or affirmation, an image, or message that seemed to rise up in prayer.

There are a few other elements of charismatic influence: For example, the music is contemporary and led by a worship band, and occasionally people will raise their hands as they sing. But it is a fairly light touch, and HTB is reluctant to describe itself as "charismatic" or even "evangelical" because they feel that such descriptions inevitably create an "us and them" atmosphere, which would hinder connecting with newcomers.

Perhaps more than introducing charismatic elements to the worship services, though, the visit of John Wimber brought another kind of openness, what I would call a kind of responsive openness. The congregation began to value more open and vulnerable relationships than had been usual before: To be able to make a warm welcome to a stranger or even genuinely get to know another person in the church can sometimes take a surprising amount of energy, but they have come to value and encourage this approach. (In case we think this is peculiar to England, I know of one woman who attended an Episcopal church in the Pacific Northwest regularly for seven years and in that time had only seen the inside of another member's house once. She is not an irregular attender or marginal Christian, being a lay theologian and professor of theology! Another young woman I know reports that she attended her local church in Ohio for more than a year and a half, and in that time only two people spoke to her.)

But even more than interpersonal openness, HTB manifests a notable openness to God. At just the point where one might be tempted to sit back and say "we're successful, things seem to be going well, we've got the model and the method set," HTB seems keen to keep learning, keep working, keep seeking out what God is calling them to do.

Their focus on evangelism reflects this commitment. Rather than say "this is just the way we do things," they relentlessly and continuously discern how their services need to change and improve in order to reach people, particularly the unchurched, the seeker, or those who do not yet profess Christ. There is a clear sense of mission in their priorities here.

There is also a sense of openness in their expectation that God will act: They consider their work to be welcoming and inviting, loving people and entertaining their questions, leaving room for God to work, rather than cajoling or pressuring someone to come to faith.

This openness can also be seen in their work in church planting, as I discuss later. It can be seen in their openness and responsiveness in working with the bishop of London rather than striking out on their own (as well, it can be seen in the bishop's willingness to work with them rather than quashing a church from a different party!). It can be seen in their practice of praying and asking God to come and do God's work—and then waiting instead of tacking on a few words of prayer as a formality to whatever they've already decided to do.

It can also be seen in their constant thirst to learn and grow in their approaches to the Alpha Course, letting it evolve as they "discover" it more and more.

Connecting with Seekers—the Alpha Course

Alpha History

Alpha began in 1977, created by Charles Marnham. HTB had been looking for a way to help people grow in their faith and encourage them in learning. It began with a curate and his wife hosting nice suppers in their house, to which they would invite ten people. After a good meal, they would give a talk on some aspect of the Christian faith and then open up the floor for discussion.

This was the format of Alpha for the first thirteen years. It was primarily intended for people who had already come to faith, for people who identified as Christian but who might want a little more background knowledge.

In 1990, Nicky Gumbel, a curate at HTB, took over the course. He did so reluctantly because he saw his call as being an evangelist. He wanted to focus on helping people come to faith. But he continued running the course more or less as it had been. Not long after he began leading it, he noticed that two people showed up to the course who weren't Christian, who wouldn't claim to be believers. But remaining in the course and engaging with the material, they came to faith.

This fascinated Nicky—and encouraged him.

At HTB they often say that Alpha is not an invention, it's a discovery. They mean that a course that had been designed for a different audience, with a different intent, has become the basis for Alpha—and that if they had sat down to write a course to introduce the faith to nonbelievers, they would have done something very different. To their surprise, people were coming to faith through this curriculum. Over time, the teaching has changed somewhat, but the basic format is still in place. This is in large part because they were convinced that they had discovered something (that was beyond their easy control) rather than having invented something.

In short, Nicky and HTB were convinced that they had found something that *worked*, and they didn't want to change it, lest it stop working. It was, in short, bearing fruit. As Mark Elsdon-Dew puts it, "the fruit is just astonishing, totally changed lives, that's what we've seen. And a totally changed church."[39]

Alpha Today

When the Alpha leaders introduced changes to the program, they were primarily a matter of welcome: improving the welcome at the door, providing more delicious food, using better lamps in the space to make it seem homier, installing a better sound system for the music and the message. But the content and style of Alpha changed little, so long as it was connecting with people. Mark talks about the process, saying "it's an evolution that God has brought us through since those early days; we've been learning all the way, and we still are."

From that initial group of ten meeting over dinner, Alpha has grown to be present in 169 countries. Twenty-four million people have been on the course since it began in 1993. It's been translated into 112 different languages, and it runs in all sorts of different churches around the world.

The impact of Alpha on the Church of England is unmistakable, as more and more bishops, clergy, theological educators, thousands of laypeople, and even Archbishop of Canterbury Justin Welby, have gone through the course and found it to be a significant part of their way into faith in Jesus. The program's tenets of hospitality, of sharing stories and learning about the faith in community, have become woven into the ethos of many congregations, which in turn has led to remarkable growth.

Alpha Format

The specifics of hospitality for the Alpha Course vary somewhat from place to place, but the course generally begins with food, whether a meal or a nice dessert and coffee. Music or another segue is offered before the next part of the course. This format shows that people care and it demonstrates hospitality, and especially for evening groups in which people might be coming from work, it allows them to attend without needing to worry about dinner.

After dinner and music comes a talk, in which some aspect of the Christian faith is explored. The talks are closely scripted, but delivered in a natural, conversational style. If guests miss a week, each talk is available online for free to allow them to catch up. There are fifteen talks in all, which are designed to be done in eleven weeks, including a day or weekend away as a group. Talks last about a half an hour total and assume no particular knowledge of the Bible or the Christian faith. Topics range from "Is there more to life than this?" (week one) to "Who is Jesus?" (week two) to "How and why should I pray?" (week five) to "Does God heal today?" (week nine) to "How can I resist evil?" (week thirteen).

After the talk, the gathering divides up into small groups; these groups form on the first night and generally stick together through the entire course. At this stage at HTB, the groups are served coffee, tea, and biscuits, but this is not the case in every setting.[40] The groups feature one host, a helper or two, and a portion of guests. The small group is seen as the heart of the course. It provides space where people can respond to the message, ask questions, talk through issues, and get to know each other. The host and helpers are not there to provide "answers" to questions, to shut down topics, or to move the conversation in the "right" way. The host's primary task is to allow everyone the space they need to explore, ask questions, and feel welcomed. The Alpha materials suggest that a key to finding a good host for the group should be "would I be comfortable with putting my best non-Christian friend in the groups with these hosts?"[41] This is essential, not least because, although Alpha is often quite prominently advertised, most of the guests who come do so because of a personal invitation.

The four sessions that take place on the weekend away are an important part of the course. Most of the meetings take place over a few hours during the week, but these sessions are part of a time away from the usual context of the meeting. Typically, a church would take a full weekend away, with the volunteers and participants going away for a time of socializing, care and hospitality, and continuing to explore the faith through these four sessions. Some churches find it easier to schedule a single full day away instead of a weekend. One church's Alpha group might gather on its own or join with several church groups in order to pool resources. The sessions might be held at a retreat center, conference center, or campground, or even at another local church. The weekend sessions, while a good bit of work to host, are intended not only to be a retreat and teaching session but also to be fun and provide opportunities to get to know people and make friends.

The talks on the weekend deal with the Holy Spirit and God's work in our lives. In line with HTB's seeking to let God work, this is seen as a time where space is created for people to encounter the Holy Spirit. Many people are committed to praying for those participating in the weekend, praying "Holy Spirit come." Experientially, this has been a time where people have been touched, often in surprising ways. Most of those who come to faith on Alpha do so on the weekend. As one leader put it, "We do Alpha, and the rest is up to God." Prayer is considered the foundation of Alpha.

Although inevitably the Alpha Course reflects much of what HTB has learned over the years, along with their own convictions, they have also worked hard to make it ecumenical and have done so through extensive conversation with Roman Catholics, Orthodox, Pentecostals, and mainline Protestants. The fruit of this consultation is that the course is now used by each of these churches in various places around the world. In my own neighborhood, the Roman Catholic church is running an Alpha Course right now; one of those attending the course is an ELCA pastor who is getting ideas so that he can run it in his own congregation.

While Alpha materials are copyrighted, they are also given away freely to anyone who would like to run the course—and everything is available for free online, including videos of the talks on sites such as YouTube and Vimeo.[42] In addition, Alpha strongly recommends that any group putting on Alpha offer it to people free of charge, including food, to keep with the emphasis on hospitality and care for guests.

Alpha Focus

HTB is clear in the focus of their work with Alpha—and evangelism generally—they seek to appeal to the 24-year-old male. This might sound surprising—and narrow, maybe even sexist. But their philosophy is that they're trying to reach the *least likely* person to be involved with church and be engaged with the Christian faith. If they can reach these folks, the thinking goes, then they can reach others as well.

The statistics show that people between the ages of 18 and 30 are less likely to be practicing Christians but also much more likely to be receptive to investigating the Christian faith than at other times of life. HTB sees that folks in this age range are searching and open, and they offer Alpha as a venue in which they can consider Christianity and make up their minds. Young people in this age group are probably not practicing Christians, and a significant number have not grown up with any Christian faith at all. For many, Alpha is their first encounter with "real, live Christians," their first direct exposure to the Christian message—and may even be their first time inside a church building.

Another component is the location for Alpha. While it often meets in a church building, the location is entirely flexible, with Alpha Courses offered in cafés, pubs, university multi-purpose rooms, on the beach, or at someone's home. Many groups have run the course in prisons, and HTB has even created a ministry called Caring For Ex-Offenders, which matches up people coming out of prison with local churches to make it easier to re-enter society. They have found that this can be an effective way of caring for people, helping them to re-establish their lives and avoid recidivism.

Alpha as Formation

A priest I knew who was learning about Alpha—and wasn't entirely convinced of its value—asked: "Why haven't they created a Beta course yet?" This is a natural question. And I imagine that HTB would encourage him to do so, if this was his calling!

But I believe there is a reason why they haven't created a series of courses all the way through Omega. While the intention is that people go to one Alpha Course, rather than coming back again and again, HTB is also very clear in its communications that they don't take peoples' phone numbers, e-mail, or surface mail addresses—they won't follow up to ask where you've been if you've stopped coming. The idea is to make the course completely welcoming and accessible to anyone who might be interested, even if you've had a bad experience with the church in the past. Taking contact information might be interpreted as pressure or a prelude to harassing someone. And so they have no real statistics on whether people return to repeat the course or join another church.

The hope, however, is that if someone comes to faith, they return to Alpha, not as a guest, but as a helper, and eventually a host. In fact, even if someone hasn't come to faith but expresses a desire to repeat Alpha, HTB will encourage the person to return as a helper. This suggests that Christian faith is not a matter of taking progressively more advanced "courses" from A to Z but rather of living out one's faith in service, of sharing what we've been given. The emphasis is on an active faith, in blessing others with the same care and hospitality that you have received. There isn't an aversion to further learning, but the Alpha Course philosophy sees learning and reflection as flowing out of action.

In fact, opportunities for further learning are encouraged. HTB established St. Paul's Theological Centre in 2005 in order to provide theological resources for the church and the Alpha Course. In addition, they offer a School of Theology course for people to grow deeper in their faith and to learn more about the Bible and theology. The course is open to anyone, whether a seasoned Christian, or someone new to the faith and looking for a "Beta" course. The format of the sessions echoes Alpha: Evenings begin with dinner, move to corporate worship, then a talk, and finish with group discussion.

St. Paul's Theological Centre, along with the North Thames Ministerial Training Course, is one of the founding partners of St. Mellitus Theological College. Begun in 2007, St. Mellitus—named after the first bishop of London—has swiftly grown to become one of the largest training centers for Anglicans in the world. They host around 210 ordinands, and more than 400 other students participate in its range of programs: There are five locations across England, with another site in Kuala Lumpur. One innovative aspect of this program is that, unlike other residential programs, students seeking ordination are involved in and employed by a church or other mission context throughout their studies; there is a different balance of parish work and formal education. So students are engaged in substantial ministry while taking classes one day a week, spending a day each week studying, and then being away for seven residential weekends and one full residential week each year. This pattern of education allows students to balance street-level experience and engagement with advanced study and reflection. Bishops report being impressed with this preparation for ministry. I would like to point out that it continues, on a larger scale, the same expectation implicit in the Alpha Course: the Christian life is an active one, engaged with the world, and education is intended to assist and fulfill that engagement.

\+ + +

Several times each year, I take groups to HTB to experience worship and to sit in on an Alpha Course. If we're interested in the growth in the Diocese of London and elsewhere, it would be irresponsible to leave this out since it's a huge part of the story. Nevertheless, some students, who are often in training for ministry, or others already ordained, will express that HTB—the screens, the music, whatever—isn't their cup of tea. I understand.

I say several things in response. First, the way the service is structured isn't *for* them. The people who go on my course in London tend to be persuaded Christians, for whom the traditional church service is working *really well*. HTB looks at this and says that there are plenty of churches like that already. They're trying to do something different, to reach folks who aren't already present. I say a little more about this in the next chapter on church planting. But the point is to remember that the main purpose of the church is not to meet its members' needs, but, as Archbishop William Temple put it, the church "exists for the benefit of those who are not its members."

Second, in terms of musical style and aesthetic choices, some people pause because they think that these are somehow the main thing. They don't want to change but suspect that maybe they might need to. This might feel threatening to them. But there is nothing sacred or inviolable about these particular choices, and HTB is likely to continue making changes as one generation rolls into another. The important thing is not aping HTB—or any other church—but worshiping God authentically in your own context and doing so in ways that strangers and newcomers can find their place and join their voice with yours. As we will see in the next chapter, HTB has been learning this in the process of church planting.

Finally, thinking of Alpha, when I look around on a Wednesday evening in a church packed with people who are uncommitted but who have come to explore the Christian faith, I'm impressed. I can think of nothing that my local church does that even comes close to this. One student said that this sort of thing would be a total non-starter at her church. I can understand why. But the question is, if Alpha isn't what you want to use yourself, what else can you do instead? How can you connect with unchurched or de-churched people in your area? How can you love and care about those people? How can you present the Christian faith, offer a gentle invitation, allow people space to question and explore, and give God space to work? How is God calling you to offer a credible witness to the gospel?

Chapter 5
Sowing the Seeds of Growth: Church Planting

A great deal of the growth in the Diocese of London has come through church planting. Often in America, church planting takes place as a brand-new congregation is begun from scratch. Most often, the church planters meet in a rented space until, ultimately, they buy some property and construct a new facility. Church planting figures heavily in the life and growth in the Diocese of London but virtually never in this form.

Instead, church planting is a partnership between the diocese and a local congregation; in the Church of England, it is not something done in isolation. The diocese provides guidance and permission, while local congregations provide other resources. It is a team effort, coordinated among various stakeholders.

Church planting also takes many forms. In its most recent vision statement, Capital Vision 2020, the diocese committed to "create or renew 100 worshiping communities" from 2013 to 2020. As I mentioned earlier, this audacious goal sets a pace of more than one new start per month! Bishop Pete Broadbent, as part of the diocese's church planting strategy, set out ten common models for church planting in London.[43]

Before turning to these models, it is important to remember that in the Church of England, "parish" is a geographical term for the neighborhood or other area in which the church is situated. A church has a parish, but in practice only a small fraction of those who reside in the parish are members of the parish church. Residents of the parish may be Baptist, Muslim, Hindu, atheist, disinterested, or otherwise uninvolved in the church. In what follows, it is useful to keep this distinction in mind. Here are the ten models that Bishop Broadbent discusses:

1. **Parish intra-congregational plant:** This model develops a new service in an existing church in order to reach new people, resulting in a new congregation meeting in the same church. As an example, some churches have started services intended to reach young adults and students, scheduled later in the day, often with different liturgical forms than other services. Although St. Paul's, Hammersmith, is itself a church plant, one of their first decisions was to begin something new intended for just this demographic: The service meets at 6 p.m. on Sundays and is a substantial congregation in its own right. Likewise, a buggy mass (a mid-morning service for preschool aged children and their caregivers) or Messy Church, as in St. Nicholas, Poplar, is an example of this (I return to St. Nicholas in chapter seven).

2. **Church plant by a congregation into their own parish:** In this model, a church starts a new congregation in its own neighborhood (parish) in order to connect with unreached people. This new plant may meet in a church or chapel structure in the area, but unless such a building is available, the congregation is more likely to meet in a community center or similar place. St. Ann's, Tottenham, which I discuss later in

this chapter, has planted two congregations in their own parish this way. Also in Tottenham, in 2010 at St. Mary's, they reopened a chapel building in their parish that had not hosted church services since the 1930s, and named it The Good Shepherd Church.

3. **Congregational graft:** A team of people from a larger, healthier church in a different parish "graft" into an existing congregation. This brings new DNA to the existing DNA of the place as well as infusing fresh energy to that church's ministry. In this model, some change of the existing church is intended, but overall it works more as partnership between old and new. In practice, this often means a "cross-tradition" church plant in which more than one form of churchmanship is offered in a single place. St. Peter's, Bethnal Green, which I discuss below, is a good example of this form of church plant.

4. **Congregational plant:** This form might be the best known and reflected in some of the most dramatic stories, although it is less likely to be reproduced going forward. Here, a leader and a congregation are sent to a church building that has been closed for some time or sent to an existing congregation that is set to be closed. In this case, the church is essentially restarted, with a new program, new congregation, and new leaders. I detail St. Paul's, Shadwell, later in this chapter, and it is a good example of this model. St. Paul's, Hammersmith, is also an example of this form of plant.

5. **Network church:** A network church creates a new church in a new space (typically rented, not intended as a fixed location through the week). Rather than focus on a place, as a parish church is, a network church draws people from around the city through relationships.

These are often located near transport nodes such as railway stations. Archdeacon Luke Miller of the Diocese of London observed that network churches tend to move in one of two directions: either they exist for a finite period of time, perhaps ceasing as people move or their lives change, or they transform gradually into a parish church, being more settled, more place-bound, and reaching people beyond the relationships that first brought the congregation together. Either of these outcomes is fine, but it suggests that a network church, in the context of London, is most likely a transitional form of church for people.

King's Cross Church, or KXC, which I mentioned briefly in chapter three, is a fine example of a network church. Planted by St. Mary's, Bryanston Square, in 2010, King's Cross Church expresses the vision for their ministry as being called "to recklessly give themselves away to God, each other, and the people of King's Cross and beyond." Their Sunday services (they have three) meet in the mornings at a primary school and in the afternoons and evenings at The Ethiopian Church. Both locations are a very short walk from King's Cross Station, a major transport hub for London. During the week, groups meet in homes and pubs.

6. **Third place church:** This model of church plant features a congregation being started in a non-sacred third space, such as a school, café, or pub. The term "third place" comes from the shape of our usual life: home is the "first" place and work the "second." Third places, according to urban sociologist Ray Oldenburg, are anchors of community life and foster broader social interaction than is the case in the first or second place.[44] Other examples of a third place include coffeehouses,

barber shops, bookstores, and bars. Fresh Expressions of Church (which are less common in London than elsewhere in the Church of England) sometimes make use of third places. St. Luke's in the High Street, which I discuss in chapter eight, operates a stall on the farmers' market on Sunday mornings and hosts a Bible study in a local café. Church E20, which is being planted on a former Olympic site in London by Annie McTighe, began with a small group of worshipers who meet Tuesday nights at a café called Tina, We Salute You. (They've since relocated to another local establishment, a bakery and café called Signorelli.)

7. **Missional communities:** These small groups of Christians are commissioned to reach particular places (such as a housing development) or networks of people (such as a Somali immigrant community, or people working in fashion or the media). Missional Communities take different shapes, from a household living intentionally as disciples of Jesus in a place to simple church (ten to twenty people seeking to live missionally in a place) to networks (in which community grows around a shared interest or pursuit—sports, a book club, business, and so forth).[45] Missional communities aren't looking for dramatic growth so much as to reproduce themselves through creating more small groups of mission-minded disciples. I say more about missional communities in chapter eight.

8. **Second place church:** These worship communities are planted in workplaces. Given the typically secular nature of work, this is often difficult. Nevertheless, the diocese takes discipleship in relation to work seriously and believes in some contexts this might be possible.

9. **International and ethnic congregations:** This approach begins new congregations that are intended to serve the needs of those new to the UK or who are otherwise not served well by existing congregations, especially those whose first language is not English. One church held a weekend retreat and realized that among its members, there were twenty-seven different first languages. Even existing English-language churches might look for opportunities to start new services in non-English languages.

10. **Churches in existing unreached communities and new developments:** The ongoing growth and expansion of London provides numerous opportunities to start new churches in areas of new housing. For these plants, the diocese works strategically with developers of new housing developments. These developments usually contain a mix of high- and mid-rise apartments and condominiums, with some intended for students, some for what in the United States we call subsidized public housing, some for affordable housing, and some to be sold at market rate: They will contain perhaps ten thousand new homes overall. Part of the legal requirement of being given the right to build and sell these new homes is to dedicate a certain amount of space to what are called community facilities.

    Archdeacon Luke Miller explains that the diocese has a strategic development department made up of people trained to work in urban planning and municipal law. They proactively approach developers and propose to them that the diocese run the new community facilities, helping the developers meet their legal obligations with a partner that has a proven track record in community work. The community centers serve the whole community, but one of the uses of the facility is hosting a church. St. Francis Church and the Engine Room, at Tottenham Hale, found in chapter nine, is a prime example of this approach.

Luke says the diocese has worked to focus every decision on mission rather than maintenance. Rather than being preoccupied with how they can hold on to whatever they have and keep the status quo, the attitude is to ask: How can we do better? And how can we think "big" to do better?

That's not to suggest that traditional—"inherited"—forms of church are in disfavor. In fact, the church that Luke served as vicar is a traditional Anglo-Catholic congregation. This varied approach to church planting simply means that all forms of church are seen as part of the mission of God.

In this spirit, Luke and others I have spoken to in the diocese are very clear: It is important to be free to try out new things, and it is equally as important to have permission to fail. But it is always better to be doing something and risk failing (and thereby learn something) than to hold back from trying something for fear of failure.

But being fearless of failure does not mean going in without a plan, or shooting from the hip, as we have already seen from the diocese's emphasis on Mission Action Plans in chapter three. The work of planting new churches is done in consultation with the area bishop. Through this collaboration, the bishop offers guidance and support; it is also an opportunity for the church to develop a business plan for their finances, structures of leadership for the team, and an approach to the (legally required) provision of baptism, marriage, and burial to residents of the parish.

In addition, this consultation is important because the diocese is not interested in having churches compete with each other. It is unlikely that a charismatic evangelical church would be allowed to plant into a parish in which there is already a charismatic evangelical church; likewise, with an Anglo-Catholic church. Ideally, churches collaborate across and within liturgical styles or theological persuasions, but the bottom line is that churches should not be arguing in public against each other.

HTB planting churches

In many ways Holy Trinity Brompton lies at the root of the movement toward church planting in London. They were inspired in the 1980s by the work of C. Peter Wagner, an American theologian and key leader of the Church Growth Movement. He said that "church planting is the most effective evangelistic methodology known under heaven."[46] We've already seen their commitment to evangelism through Alpha. About the same time as that program launched, HTB began to explore church planting as another means of evangelism.

Of course, church planting in the Church of England is different than in the United States: As I mentioned earlier, every blade of grass already grows in a parish. If this is true, then in one sense all of England is spoken for and there's no room to plant new churches. Yet HTB decided they were being called not only to plant churches but also they needed to do so with the authorization and blessing of the bishop. And their bishop at the time decided that he would support them.[47]

This approach contrasts to some church planting practice in America, which tends to be more independent. In practical terms, the Diocese of London's approach means that rather than a new plant being a maverick, wildcatting for members, from the beginning they are committed to being in conversation with bishops and working with (and often, especially at first, persuading) those with whom they might not agree or who might be skeptical of HTB's approach. I cannot overstate how much HTB's decision along these lines—and the bishops' decision to work with them—has shaped and enhanced the process of church planting in London. HTB, the bishops, and the larger diocese have learned and grown through this ongoing relationship.

In 1985, after much prayer and at the bishop's invitation, HTB sent its first group of a hundred people to plant a church into St. Barnabas, Kensington, along with one of their assistant clergy, John Irving, who became the new vicar. St. Barnabas had a massive structure, built to house 800 but had been stumbling along serving around fifteen. The infusion of a large group of committed, mission-minded worshipers helped turn the church around, and it is today home to hundreds of worshipers. Subsequent plants from HTB came in 1987, 1990, and in 1994. The process has continued rolling since then, and in thirty-plus years, HTB has planted sixteen churches, many of which have gone on to plant churches of their own.

HTB found they need three things in order to plant a church: the bishop's invitation, a church building into which to plant, and an area to draw from to grow a congregation. This last point means that they will not plant into an area with another growing congregation. As Mark Elsdon-Dew of HTB says, they "are not interested in transfer growth." Consistent with their emphasis on evangelism, they seek out those who do not belong to a church.

HTB has developed a common pattern to planting churches. First, the entire process is immersed in prayer. They believe strongly that this is not simply a human activity but that they are trying to be faithful and responsive to God's leading and call. Second, historically HTB sent a team of people, ranging in number from ten to as many as 200 (but usually between thirty and fifty), to be the core of the new congregation; their current practice has moved toward sending smaller groups to join struggling congregations. Along with these, they send a team of leaders, including a priest, an administrator, a youth worker, and others as needed. A final element of the plant is a grant to help with expenses.

In sending clergy, lay leaders, and money, HTB has significant skin in the game. From this perspective, HTB and other congregations involved in planting cannot just pay lip service or passively assent. It takes commitment, and there is a cost.

Ric Thorpe became rector of St. Paul's, Shadwell, when it was grafted into by HTB, and which itself has gone on to plant several churches in only a few years. He puts it clearly: "When you plant a church, you send your best people." Ric says "send," but it is not a matter of members turning up one Sunday to be told that—surprise!—their membership has been transferred elsewhere. It is an intentional process of discernment by the whole membership of the church. The prospect of moving to a different congregation and a different neighborhood is often seen as an exciting and natural part of members' faith life. This commitment to mission, to church planting, and to responding to the call of God is instilled deeply in the congregation, so much that it has become a part of the church's DNA.

Sending a group of people gives the nascent congregation a fighting chance for success. Ric estimates that by sending a team already committed to mission and to the church, you create a critical mass of people that saves five to ten years of the initial work of planting. As the diocese's report *Another Capital Idea* puts it, "when moribund churches receive a transplanting team and reopen for business they tend to attract quite a lot of new adherents fairly quickly."[48] Further, when an empty and unused church building (or one that *appears* empty and unused) is reopened and sings with new life, it becomes an embodied sign of the Holy Spirit's work in the community and can prove very attractive.

The congregation receiving the transplant team is in a rather vulnerable position. In nearly every case, they are facing closure and the offer of receiving a transplant team is the only other option. The team comes in with authority from the bishop, and they are explicit that they are coming in to make changes. They will add services, they will reorder the church (by removing pews or installing screens and a sound system, for example), and they will bring new people and new perspectives. This is fair enough, since the church, pre-transplant, is waning. Business as usual isn't working, and so it's time to try something else or close.

At the same time, HTB's approach has evolved to be more respectful of the life of the congregation into which it is planting, particularly as the work has changed from restarting a congregation to grafting into an existing congregation looking for new life. With these in-grafting projects, they are careful to sustain the original service the church offered, in something like its original form. One example is St. Augustine's, Queensgate, an architecturally significant Gothic Revival building with historically very Anglo-Catholic worship. By 2010 it was fading and set to close. It is located very near HTB. In 2010 they were invited by the bishop to transplant in to HTB to revive St. Augustine's; in 2011 the (historically small) parish of St. Augustine's was incorporated into HTB's parish. The people of St. Augustine's allowed the pews to be removed but decided it was important for at least one Sunday morning worship service to retain its Anglo-Catholic shape. HTB agreed, saying that they would try it out for a year and see how it went. They continued this service, with incense, vestments, choir, classical mass settings, eucharist every service—all elements not generally found in an HTB service. And after a year, they found that, rather than just an in-house exercise for the few remnants from St. Augustine's, the service was growing. And so they decided to keep the service. St. Augustine's now has two more traditional services on Sunday mornings. During the week, the space is used as a day shelter, which provides "an inviting, warm, and safe space where all are welcome to enjoy a hot meal, an all-day café, haircuts, clothing, a computer bank, an arts station, and a range of other community building activities." Guests also have access to a range of support services, such as debt advice, job placement, and recovery from addiction. November through March, St. Augustine's also hosts a night shelter for those who need a place for a hot meal and shelter.[49]

This collaboration is particularly significant because one of the criticisms of HTB has been that it tends to have a static shape to the services offered: charismatic-tinged praise band in a reordered worship space, sermon for seekers, colored lights, coffee bar, young people. On the one hand, HTB is clear that they do this because it works, because it connects with people who are not typically part of the church. As Nicky Gumbel says, "I heard somewhere that around 2 percent of the population like classical music and 98 percent like modern music." Reasoning that there is a fair amount of the church that caters to the 2 percent, he thinks more churches should work to reach the 98 percent.

On the other hand, there is a question of how much of the 98 percent they reach, whether this model is too expensive for other churches to implement, whether it can work in rural areas, many suburban areas, or in areas of urban social deprivation. While those who worship at HTB, who attend Alpha, and who participate in church plants are fabulously diverse racially and ethnically, they have very often been middle or upper-middle class. This makes St. Augustine's, with its rather different churchmanship, all the more significant, as an example of how HTB can embrace other worship styles. It also makes the work of similar church plants in London's East End, such as St. Paul's, Shadwell, and St. Peter's, Bethnal Green, even more important as these churches seek to be connected to their neighborhoods, committed to both social relief and evangelism and working to create cross-tradition churches. Finally, as HTB has continued to work, pray, and reflect, this work of being invited to plant into other churches has increasingly come to be seen not as planting a new church but as partnering with an existing one.[50]

St Paul's, Hammersmith

St. Paul's, Hammersmith, occupies a large, very prominent church building that was constructed in the 1850s. It sits alongside a stretch of highway known as the Hammersmith Flyover and is obviously visible to passengers as they fly into Heathrow Airport. The structure is one of only a handful of churches that nearly all Londoners would instantly recognize: It is a landmark.

The church once boasted a congregation to match, including a youth group of around 200 young people. But it had been withering away for some time, and by 1999 only about twenty worshipers called it home. It happened that a group of people at HTB, including Simon Downham, one of their curates, had been praying about the possibility of leading a church plant somewhere. They had begun thinking about this very strategic location but had assumed that the opportunity wouldn't open up to them.

To their great surprise, after the previous vicar departed, Bishop of London Richard Chartres approached HTB to ask if they could revive the congregation. Otherwise, St. Paul's might simply have to close. In response HTB sent about 180 people, including Simon as the new vicar. With the original members who decided to stay, they began with around 190 total.

It was important that the new church plant start out with a large group. Partly, it was simply the size of the facility: They didn't want the church to appear empty. (The mean attendance on a Sunday in a London church is only around 140.) By starting out with a critical mass, they were able to leverage this group and their energy for the next stage of growth rather than trying desperately to fill the space as their first challenge. Many of those who transplanted into St. Paul's were young families who already lived in Hammersmith who had been traveling to HTB. What's more, those who came from HTB tended to be already involved in leadership at many levels, whether leading small groups, working on the PCC (vestry or church council), or serving in ordained leadership.

St. Paul's focused on high-quality work with families as part of its first stage. They began two new services, including a more charismatic-inflected, seeker-oriented Sunday evening service at 7 p.m. Through these efforts, they grew to around 550 Usual Sunday Attendance after about three years. Numbers have remained steady since. This might look like stagnation, but as we've seen with churches in other parts of London, numerical stability sometimes masks growth. Hammersmith sees a great deal of demographic churn, especially among young families, who tend to move farther out from the city as their families grow and enter school. For instance, one summer, the congregation lost 160 people who had simply moved to other neighborhoods to find larger homes. Over a five-year period, St. Paul's saw a turnover of roughly 50 percent, which means maintaining stable attendance requires constantly attracting new people and incorporating them effectively.

In addition to St. Paul's own growth, they have themselves been involved in church planting/transplanting. In 2010, St. Paul's sent fifty to sixty people into another church, St. Andrew's, Fulham. In less than a year, the congregation doubled. In addition, some members of St. Paul's have gone on to plant new congregations as far afield as Sydney and Los Angeles. The point here is not so much the numbers as the principle: Church planting—and thinking beyond merely sustaining a single congregation—has been a part of the culture of St. Paul's from its new beginning.

St. Paul's, Shadwell

On the other side of London is St. Paul's, Shadwell. Inside the building, near the front wall on the right, is a fairly nondescript table that in many ways serves as an image of the church's approach to mission.

The original church was built by Puritans in the mid-seventeenth century, although the present structure in London's East End dates to the early 1800s. Over the centuries, it has gone through many changes, from being a much more word-centered place of preaching to an Anglo-Catholic congregation and back again. Situated near the former docks area of London, it was known for a time as a place with a special ministry to sailors. Captain James Cook, a famed explorer, worshiped there, and some seventy sea captains are buried in the churchyard. The mother of U.S. President Thomas Jefferson was baptized there. There is no lack of history at St. Paul's.

There were, however, fairly few who called the church home in the past few decades: The closure of the nearby docks hastened the decline. By 2004, only around fifteen worshiped there. Some said that St. Paul's should be closed.

But the bishop and the archdeacon wanted to try something different, and so they invited HTB to consider a transplant into St. Paul's. HTB realized that around eighty people in the congregation were from the Shadwell area, young professionals with corporate employers in the new Docklands development. In addition, some twenty people volunteered to relocate to East London to be a part of the new church. And so Ric Thorpe[51], curate at HTB, became the new vicar, coming with around 100 people.

The new transplant reordered the interior, removing the pews in favor of flexible seating and installing a new sound system and projector. Removing the pews also allowed the use of the church space during the week for programs, such as morning groups for kids and their caregivers,[52] children's clubs, and a night shelter during the winter months. The church is now used throughout the week and around the clock as a place of life and outreach.

The nondescript table at the church entry is not flashy or showy. It does, however, date from 1685, well before the present building and nearly a century before the founding of America. And it captures Ric's approach to mission, which he summarizes with three phrases:

1) Honor the past
2) Navigate change in the present
3) Build for the future

The table is worn and chipped from use; it doesn't have any special value as an antique. But for every service of eucharist at St. Paul's, it is brought out into the nave, lovingly draped with a white cloth, and serves as a communion table. It is honored as a sign of continuity with the past of this congregation. At the same time, it is honored through *use* rather than being an item put on display. It is used by the congregation for its nourishment in the present, as they navigate change, rather than being "trapped in amber" as it might be in a museum. But its ultimate value might be as it helps the congregation to build for and move into the future.

From the beginning of its new, transplanted life, St. Paul's has seen itself as a church that plants churches. From the initial transplant of 100 people, it grew in ten years to become a community of 350. But as a church that plants churches, people come to belong to it with the expectation that they may well be called by God to go elsewhere as a part of their life of faith. In eleven years, they helped to transplant into three other churches, which are now themselves growing.

As part of this work of transplanting, St. Paul's is clear that one size does not fit all: Each transplant project is as individual as the church being transplanted into and the neighborhood around it. And so, when St. Peter's in Bethnal Green, historically an Anglo-Catholic church, approached St. Paul's in 2010 with the blessing of the Bishop Chartres, St. Paul's sent twenty members, including curate Adam Atkinson and his family, to join the twenty remaining members of St. Peter's. Together, the newcomers and the remainers have navigated the process of change and growth. It hasn't been a case of the new folks coming in and calling all of the shots. St. Peter's is now a thriving example of a "cross-tradition" church plant, with one service tending toward Anglo-Catholic and another new service toward charismatic. They are heavily involved in the local community and increased from the initial forty to weekly attendance of around 130-150 in 2019 —with growth in both services. They also began a Sunday evening service for younger adults that grew to about twenty. They did this in part because after about four years they reached a plateau of attendance and growth had slowed or stopped. The new service created space for growth to continue in a different service, and the other services grew by filling back up, as others took the place of those who had switched to the later service. At the time, they had a younger ordinand in training who was charged with leading the later service. After he was ordained, he, his wife, and the twenty who were part of that service were then sent out as a new church plant. (That means St. Peter's sent out a group that was roughly one-eighth of their total attendance to begin something new!)

St. Luke's, Millwall, on the Isle of Dogs is a little different. St. Luke's was actually a part of the parish of Christ Church on the Isle of Dogs rather than being its own parish. Christ Church found itself in the liberal catholic tradition of the Church of England and was healthy and sustainable, but St. Luke's in the northwest part of the parish was struggling. The church building was tumbling down, and only about fifteen people remained. A Bishop's Mission Order was put in place in 2013 that allowed a group to come into St. Luke's as a transplant, enabling it to function as a separate church from Christ Church. This was seen as strategically important because St. Luke's sits in the shadow of significant new development in and around the Docklands, which includes thousands of new housing units. Many new people, including many professionals, have moved into the area and continue to do so, and having a lively church presence was important. In addition, a wide variety of longtime, often working-class residents live on the island: There are two very different populations with distinct needs in one area.

St. Paul's sent a priest, Ed Dix, and twenty-five people. St. Luke's began worshiping in space rented from the local school and began a series of activities intended to make connections with the local community. Ed says that their priority was to give things away to folks in the neighborhood so that the church's generosity mirrored God's—God gives without expecting repayment! Their outreach to the area includes a boxing club for at-risk youth. St. Luke's has grown in a couple of years to around seventy on a typical Sunday. They have built—and in November 2018—opened a new church building on the site of the old one. St. Luke's has returned to being a parish in its own right, independent of Christ Church.

The exact shape and method of transplanting into the Isle of Dogs was different from the transplant into St. Peter's, Bethnal Green, and different from another transplant St. Paul's undertook into All Hallows, Bromley-by-Bow. But even as the methods and forms are distinct to the particular communities, Ric insists on a common principle: To plant another church, you must send your best people. This is not a way to get rid of marginal or inconvenient members. Church planting is an opportunity to give away those who have the most energy and vision to bless another congregation. This means that church planting is a costly proposition!

It is all the more costly for St. Paul's because, as we have seen with other churches, they routinely lose about a third of their congregation to demographic churn each year as families and young adults move. Yet they have found that the people sent out to other congregations end up being replaced and the sending church regenerates itself. Ric found that within a year of sending out planters, St. Paul's grew by about 25 percent.

As a final word, in case it sounds as if St. Paul's is solely focused on growth and planting, it is worth mentioning that Ric's focus is planning for a new generation, thinking twenty-five years out, not only for the church but also for the neighborhood. Given that Shadwell is a very mixed neighborhood, with highly educated professionals and the second highest concentration of child poverty in the country, he is focused on what the church can do. He speaks with passion: "*On our watch*, can we do something about child poverty?" He is involved in the life of the neighborhood because "to love your neighbor, you have to *meet* your neighbor!" Ric and other community leaders are working to attract and retain affordable housing and improve the local schools. Ric has also found that some people coming to St. Paul's are choosing to move into Shadwell, to become rooted in the community, committing to settle there as missionaries and working for the good of their neighbors.

These HTB church plants are an important part of the story of how the diocese has gotten to this point. But they are not the only way to plant a church—and even this model of church planting is changing.

St Ann's, Tottenham

We met John Wood in chapter two. He and St. Ann's in Tottenham have grown a large leadership team from folks in the community—some volunteers and some paid. They have also developed a different model of church planting than HTB, one that might work especially well for less well-endowed churches or those working in poorer areas.

One report styled this model of church planting as a "minster model." It relies on a central church that can provide "collegial support to a team of church leaders based in that church or in attached churches over a geographical area."[53] These new congregations might meet at the central church or across other sites, often within the same parish.

And so St. Ann's has begun one congregation in a portable structure in the Tiverton housing development, called Church@TheHut. It started another on the Broadwater Farm Estate, called Church on the Farm, which likewise meets in a structure that might otherwise serve as a portable classroom.

All the facilities are rented, and the space at Tiverton is shared with other groups; it's not specifically dedicated to being a church structure.

St. Ann's, along with St. Mary's, Tottenham, has also been a large part of beginning The Engine Room community center and St. Francis' Church at the Hale Village development on redeveloped industrial land. This is an interesting example of cross-party participation, as St. Ann's describes itself as Pentecostal evangelical, while St. Mary's is traditional Anglo-Catholic. We hear more about The Engine Room and St. Francis's Church, the first new purpose-built church to be opened in London in forty years, in chapter nine.

In planting churches, John Wood writes: "It's important to begin with listening to the local people and build relationships before starting worship services." This is especially critical in an area such as Tottenham, which is often described as poor or socially deprived. John and others suggest that all too often, the government or others bent on doing good come into a neighborhood with all kinds of solutions to what they perceive as the problem but little appetite for the work of building relationships with actual people. Being "in" and "of" Tottenham is central to St. Ann's.

As with St. Paul's, Shadwell, St. Ann's commitment to growth and evangelism might suggest that the church is less committed to matters of justice in the community. This is far from the case. Among St. Ann's many ministries is Hope in Tottenham, a charitable social enterprise that has garnered national attention and a number of awards. The community-based initiative is staffed by local people and draws from a wide volunteer base. With a mission to improve community cohesion and resilience, its four programs have been praised for being high impact and low cost. A school counseling program involves nearly thirty local schools and employs around twenty counselors, mostly part-time. The program is self-funding, supported by the schools, and with a budget of about half as much as comparable programs. Counselors work with students on a wide range of issues including bereavement and social and emotional difficulties. The program arose out of a conversation John had with a local principal about a specific situation that the city's mental health services simply couldn't handle quickly enough. A second program brings together local police recruits and youth to hear from each other. The discussions have been frank: Police have learned what young people expect of them, and the teens have been surprised by the pressures facing the police. Other programs with Hope in Tottenham include youth work and a mentoring program for work placement. Key to the program's success is its grassroots understanding and approach to street-level struggles in the neighborhood, and, just as importantly, it involves local people working to improve their own lives.[54]

St. Ann's has planted various congregations within its own parish. They are small congregations but deeply connected to a specific part of Tottenham. Each new plant begins with listening and relationship building. Indigenous leaders are identified and raised up for the work. These communities of faith are vibrant, active, and engaged; they are also sustainable, requiring little overhead. The priority for John and St. Ann's is that the work is local and self-supporting. The growth of St. Ann's and its several congregations is rooted in their commitment to listen, be present, and reach out with the gospel message to those who are not already there. Even while other models have seen substantial numerical growth, this indigenous, modest, sustainable model of church planting might be within the reach of a wider variety of congregations in London.

New Models

Although HTB and the diocese worked together on a number of larger church plants or restarts, with the start of Capital Vision 2020 the model moved to focus more on smaller transplants and starting smaller communities.

While the goal is 100 new worshiping communities by 2020, these communities will by no means look the same. The Centre for Church Planting suggests that these new worshiping communities will comprise:

A. Three newly built churches, as part of newer developments

B. Twelve closed church buildings reopening as churches. (Interestingly, this has become more difficult, because after a number of such reopenings, they are running out of closed churches! Instead, the diocese is increasingly deciding not to renew leases of groups who have rented former church properties for other functions.)

C. Ten transplants, in which a group is sent from one church to another to bring new life and growth—but these groups will be smaller than the groups sent previously, closer to twenty or thirty than 100 (as in St. Paul's, Shadwell).

D. Ten new worshiping communities begun in Church of England schools

E. Fifteen worshiping communities (likely missional communities) in social housing projects, which have long been neglected by the church

F. Fifteen other missional communities at work with particular places throughout London, especially focused on new groups not otherwise in the church and languages not widely present in the church

G. Ten new worshiping communities especially focused on employment sectors such as artists, entertainers, or those employed in the fashion industry

H. Five new network churches (meeting within parish boundaries but not themselves a part of the parish, often found on the edge or seam of one parish and another)

I. Twenty new services begun at existing churches, doing things in a new way to reach new people. This often involves starting a new service at a new time or a new day and may involve a language or ethnic group not otherwise represented in the congregation.

Overall, this audacious vision for new worshiping communities takes a slightly different approach to church planting, moving away from transplanting large groups from one church to help restart another and toward smaller-scale efforts, in multiple directions at once, in order to reach as many people as possible with the gospel. They are new churches to reach new people in new ways.

In case this is beginning to sound like empire building or an effort to reclaim a golden age of Christendom, consider this: Roughly 4.3 million people live within the boundaries of the Diocese of London. Of these, about 8 percent are involved in a church of some kind; those in a Church of England congregation represent about 1.7 percent, a tiny fragment of the whole city.

The staff at the Centre for Church Planting are crystal clear about their priority: They are starting new churches and worshiping communities in order to reach the 92 percent not already involved in a church, not to "steal sheep" from other denominations. They also point out that, if every one of these 100 new worshiping communities thrives and grows to its envisioned size, the percentage of people worshiping in a Church of England context in London will grow from 1.7 percent to 1.8 percent!

Conclusion

A wide range of activities in the Diocese of London fall under the heading of church planting. Some are small scale, while others involve creating new churches where previous ones had closed. All have brought new life and growth to churches in the diocese, both those who have sent people and those who have received them.

Five elements of these stories stand out as worth emphasizing as we consider church planting. The first is that church planting is something done intentionally. Nobody plants a church, in any form, by accident. The churches we've met in this chapter made church planting a part of their identity. Sometimes it is as explicit as St. Paul's, Shadwell, whose tagline is that they are a church that plants churches. But in every case, congregations have begun not because people backed into the activity but because they prayed, planned, persuaded, strategized, listened, conferred, and collaborated over the course of a year or more.

Further, planting a new congregation requires commitment from the leadership and membership. In quite a number of these stories, a congregation sent a portion of its membership—often some of their strongest core members—to graft into an existing congregation. The endeavor requires time, energy, and money, whether a small-scale plant like Church@TheHut or a large restart like St. Paul's, Hammersmith. Church planting is costly.

Despite the cost, churches in London display a remarkable and uncommon willingness to try new things and risk failing, rather than playing it safe and protectively trying to hold on to whatever they have. This attitude is pervasive, even among churches whose numbers are holding steady rather than growing, often the result of annual turnover of 30 percent or more. This resilience and entrepreneurial creativity serve them well.

Church planting in London is also contextual. While there are some specific models, it is clear that there is not one single way that things must be done. Some models work better in some areas and with certain populations than others. Church on the Farm is different from St. Luke's on the Isle of Dogs, and both are different from St. Augustine's, Queensgate. There isn't one model of church planting anymore than there is one form of church. The context of the church plant and its envisioned population are what shape the form of the new congregation, not some prescribed, cookie-cutter approach.

Finally, church planting activities in London are adaptive. This is evident in the planting efforts by HTB (and their daughter congregations) over several decades. They began in one way and continually modify the process through discernment, listening, and learning. Where one style of music may have dominated before, there is now a greater openness to other forms; where a church graft may have represented a single tradition before, now the church graft is a partnership between newcomers and those who remain; where a particular emphasis on evangelism and the Alpha Course might have been at the fore, now this priority is often paired with a concern for the wider welfare of the city and its people. And as more models of church planting have been embraced, the church can take different forms for different people in different places.

Chapter 6
Fanning the Flame: Catholic Growth

A fair amount of the growth that we've discussed to this point has been found in more evangelical and charismatic churches. But historically the Diocese of London has been a bastion of more catholic expressions of Anglicanism. Churches such as All Saints', Margaret Street; St. Mary's, Primrose Hill; Holy Trinity, Sloane Square; the "Twelve Apostles" of London's East End; and even St. Paul's Cathedral have been marked by a deep catholic piety. Since the rise of Anglo-Catholicism in the nineteenth century, many congregations in London have found their identity in the celebration of high mass, ornamented by incense, solemn choirs, elaborate vestments, devotions to St. Mary ("Our Lady") including the rosary, in Gothic Revival and Baroque architecture, and in elaborate processions, including Corpus Christi processions and the "beating of the bounds" undertaken by churches since the Middle Ages. Even today, a few traditionalist priests in London look askance at the ordination of women, and some roll their eyes at what they might call the "happy clappy" services of the charismatics. Indeed, a previous bishop of London, after stepping down in 1991, entered the Roman Catholic ministry. The catholic identity of the Diocese of London runs deep, even today.[55]

Catholic identity for Anglicans ranges from more traditional catholic to liberal catholic, with a few positions in-between. These groups share a great deal in common, including more traditional patterns of worship services and a conviction that the sacraments ought to be central to the life of the parish church. Over the last half century, one issue that has divided the groups has been the ordination of women, embraced by more liberal catholics but not by traditionalists. Indeed, London was one of the few dioceses that voted against the ordination of women in the early 1990s. While a few leaders remain today who do not support the ordination of women—including one, a vicar of a thriving, growing church, who was made a bishop in 2014—that is not diocesan policy. In fact, the former bishop of London, Richard Chartres, says that the energy expended over these disputes fueled an "intense factional strife which militated against any common action."[56] Being caught up in and distracted by this debate (resolved by an act of General Synod in 1993 to allow women to be ordained) diffused energy that could otherwise be dedicated to mission. Further proof that the diocese has a different position on the ordination of women is Bishop Richard's successor: Bishop of London Sarah Mullally.

That issue having been resolved, the categories become a bit murkier: I've met women priests who identify enthusiastically as catholic but would not call themselves "liberal catholic." Because of this murkiness—and because it is not my intent to be a cheerleader for a party but for growth in many different forms—I include in this chapter a number of leaders and churches that fall into the broad category of "catholic" without further identifying them as "traditional" or "liberal" or in-between.

The Centre for Theology and Community completed a study in late 2017 of growth in catholic churches, entitled *A Time to Sow*. The study focused on seven parishes in London, from both the Diocese of London and the Diocese of Southwark. It found churches growing gently, at about five to ten percent a year, at both traditional services and new midweek services. Most of them have also, over the same time, noted increased levels of giving. Moreover, all seven of the churches are within some of the most deprived demographic areas of the country. This suggests that growing churches are not only the province of the middle class: The church grows with all sorts of people from all walks of life.[57]

The report distills seven practices common in these growing Anglo-Catholic churches:

1) Growth-minded priests: Clergy leadership are intentional and committed to growth as part of their ministry

2) Maximizing resources: Assets, particularly property, are used proactively for the church's ministry or to bring in revenue

3) Building leadership capacity: Lay leaders, volunteers, and interns are valued and equipped for their ministry; although ordained leadership is valued, the priest does not jealously guard the ministry of the church

4) Hospitality: Each church works intentionally to be welcoming to newcomers while also maintaining a beautiful traditional liturgy; this includes a focus on welcoming folks and offering coffee and refreshments following the services

5) Children included: Each church features programs on Sundays and/or during the week for children

6) Open to working with local partners: These growing churches are connected to their local schools and other

community organizations, continually looking for opportunities to serve alongside others and to be visibly involved in local life beyond the church walls

7) Midweek encounters: These churches all feature opportunities for those outside the church to enter and get to know church members or the clergy, such as a caregivers and children group. These types of activities provide space for conversation and a "porous" quality to the church for the community[58]

The report also emphasized that these churches were not growing because of incredibly creative and innovative, out-of-the-box programs. On the contrary, "it seems that the challenge is rarely to invent a brand-new activity but to do simple things well and be open to learning from the habits of others."[59]

Holy Trinity Sloane Square

Holy Trinity Sloane Square is located in Chelsea, walking distance from (the rather different) Holy Trinity Brompton, which we explored earlier. The building, completed in 1890, was called the "Cathedral of the Arts & Crafts Movement" by one-time poet laureate, Sir John Betjeman, and contains works by notable artists of that movement, including stained glass by Edward Burne-Jones and William Morris. This beautiful structure has been nearly lost three times: once, when it was struck by German bombs in World War II; again in the 1960s, when the estate that owns the land the church sits on took steps to raze it and replace it with a smaller structure as part of a housing development (the wrecking ball was averted by the intervention of Betjeman[60] and the Victorian Society); and then finally at the beginning of the tenure of Bishop Richard Chartres.

Bishop Richard tells that when he was appointed, one of the first papers he received was an order to close Holy Trinity Sloane Square. The area's archdeacon called the neighborhood "impermeable," noting that the previous rector had become quite depressed at the lack of response to the church's ministry. Despite the beauty of the structure, the consensus was that there was no possibility for sustainable ministry. Bishop Richard says that as the diocese researched the issue, they found that they would not realize a profit on the sale of the (rather valuable) real estate, since it would revert to the estate of the Cadogan family.[61]

Instead of going along with the consensus, Bishop Richard took a measured risk. In 1997, he appointed Bishop Michael Marshall, one-time bishop of Woolwich in the Diocese of Southwark, as priest-in-charge. An energetic and talented leader, Bishop Michael restored a more elaborate, catholic style of worship and insisted on keeping the church's doors open all day to the community as well as sponsoring and supporting art and music. Over the ten years of his ministry, Holy Trinity moved from being on the brink of closure to a vibrant congregation of more than 300, including a thriving program with children and families.

A neighboring church, St. Saviour, Upper Chelsea, also had been struggling, when Rob Gillion was called to serve there in 1999. The area bishop encouraged him to be creative in his work. Rob and Janine, his wife, had both worked as actors before Rob entered the ministry. They began dreaming of a ministry at the intersection of the church and the stage. They created a theatre church at St Saviour's, calling it Intermission. Originally intended to be a support network for Christian artists, it quickly grew into something much larger, incorporating Intermission Theatre, Intermission Youth Theatre, Intermission Outreach, and Intermission Pictures. In addition, principal Sunday services were moved to Sunday evenings, and the church's music is supported by the West End Gospel Choir, which is pleased to make their home at St. Saviour's.

The Intermission Youth Theatre (IYT) has particularly made a splash. It engages at-risk youth from inner-city neighborhoods. IYT began in 2008 to work with youth who were offenders with a record, or else at risk of offending, or who otherwise didn't have many opportunities. The program continues today, taking on twenty-five young people, ages fifteen to twenty-five each year. The group works with Shakespearean drama, adapting it with the young people to contemporary language and conditions. Developed to help young people grow in their creativity and confidence and to bolster their hopes and ambitions, the program culminates each year with a four-week professional run of the dramatic piece they adapted.

And the work of IYT is integrated with the work of St Saviour's. Rob began what he called Pause for Thought, an opportunity for the actors to engage scripture, prayer, and worship in order to explore their relationship with God. The participants in IYT come from various areas, faiths, and nationalities. But the IYT is a Christian ministry. As Artistic Director Darren Raymond put it, "Jesus is at the center of everything we do. It's about relationships, and we're trying to bring them closer to Christ. The way I see the young people change is amazing. People are blown away by the show, but I'm blown away by how much they change."[62]

In 2008, Rob was invited to become rector of Holy Trinity Sloane Square as well, and in 2011, the two churches combined. Three years later, Rob was elected bishop of Riverina in Australia and was succeeded in 2015 by Canon Nicholas Wheeler. Nicholas came to Chelsea after serving as priest for several years in the City of God in Rio de Janeiro, Brazil. But before that, he was vicar at St. Michael's, Camden

Town (which we glanced at in chapter two) and helped to move them from being struggling and inward-looking to engaging with the surrounding community. Under his leadership, Holy Trinity and St. Saviour's continue to have thriving ministries.

St. Mary The Virgin, Tottenham

The parish of St. Mary's in Tottenham was founded in 1884 and the church structure built not long after. It was established as many moved into the newly developed area. The first decades were an energetic time of building and growth, which included a new church hall, vicarage, and a hall for the Church Lads' Brigade. The parish also founded a mission church. Growth continued up until the first World War, with up to 900 communicants at Easter.

Between the wars, involvement flagged, and periods of modest growth, stagnation, and decline punctuated the post-war period, until it very nearly closed in the 1980s. But new life began percolating up around that time as the church became much more intentional in reaching out to and connecting with the West Indian immigrants who were increasingly making their homes in the neighborhood. Growth continued under Luke Miller, who became vicar in 1994. Attendance continued to grow under Luke's ministry, and, after he departed to become archdeacon of Hampstead in 2011, under his successor, Simon Morris. Although numbers do not yet match those heady decades, the most recent numbers for attendance at Easter services were the highest since 1937.

So, what has driven this new life and growth at St. Mary's?

When Luke Miller became the vicar, he threw himself into a church-growth mode. He followed what he calls the traditional pastoral model: get to know people's names, love and care for them wherever they were, visit them at home, and so forth. This kind of "retail" evangelism more than doubled average Sunday attendance over the seventeen years he served there.

But this priest-centered pastoral model is demanding and can also be exhausting—not to mention that a priest can only make so many relational connections in the community, and so the growth can be limited. Luke's successor Simon moved to a broader, program-based model: It retains a great deal of pastoral emphasis but is less dependent on a single clergyperson for this work, drawing on the gifts and callings of laypeople to work alongside the sacramental ministry of the priest.

Second, the church's community presence has been a key part of the growth. Luke focused on restoring the church's facilities. Through ordinary wear and tear and a bit of neglect, much of the property needed renewing, including several halls throughout the parish that the church owned. Their physical improvement became a sign to the community that the church was still filled with life, not decaying and dying. The remodeled facilities hosted community functions such as moms and toddlers' groups, offering an amenity for the neighborhood as well as bringing in some much-needed funds.

St. Mary's ongoing commitment to being in and with the community was clearly on display in 2011, when a series of riots shook Tottenham. (I say more about the riots in chapter ten.) Widespread burning and looting savaged the neighborhood, including a very large carpeting store across the street from the church, which spectacularly burned to the ground. The fire became a symbol of the riots. It also displaced the thirty families who lived above the shop.

The folks at St. Mary's jumped into action. They helped the homeless and emergency personnel. Using the available electricity, they offered tea and coffee, food, a place to sit, a toilet, a friendly face, and sympathetic ear. They boiled kettles of water for people for their homes. And they gave somewhere that they could charge their mobile phones, especially important since landlines are uncommon in the area.

Perhaps most crucially, all of this happened spontaneously, led by the members of the church. Simon, the recently installed vicar, had been away leading a group on pilgrimage. He returned early to be with his people in the aftermath only to find the church's response was already in full swing. This meant that rather than boiling water in the church hall, Simon could be walking around the neighborhood, checking on how people were doing, and listening to what else the church might do to help. Although people in Tottenham usually greeted clergy on the street, in the wake of the riots, Simon said people engaged him much more in conversation. Because he had already spent time walking the streets and being a part of the neighborhood, he was a trusted resource in a time of crisis.[63] His response—and St. Mary's—was not something special or unusual but simply a part of being in and of Tottenham. When the neighborhood suffers, the church suffers with it—and works to address that suffering.

Another component of St. Mary's growth stems from their church planting efforts. When Luke was vicar, he realized that the church still owned a facility where St. Mary's had planted a mission church decades before. That church had closed in the 1930s. After a period of community engagement, to gauge interest and see what was needed in the area, St. Mary's decided to reopen the mission with the name The Good Shepherd Church. After nearly eighty years of not hosting Christian worship, the chapel reopened in September 2010. They are now a vital church community, a part of the parish of St. Mary the Virgin, offering a Sunday evening service and a Tuesday morning service that together draw around fifty people.

Strategies and factors in catholic growth

I earlier used the phrase "retail evangelism." By this, I mean the labor-intense work of meeting people one by one and inviting them to church and into faith in Jesus. This is good and valuable work, so long as we see this as the work of the whole church and not just the clergy.

This "retail evangelism" might be contrasted with the more "wholesale evangelism" of the Alpha Course, which is also rooted in relationship but brings in larger groups of the uncommitted or skeptical at the same time to consider the gospel. Alpha can effectively advertise on buses and billboards and reach a great many at once. Both approaches have an important role to play in the life of the church.

But to be clear: Evangelism is not only for evangelicals. Some approaches to evangelism fit well with a more Anglo-Catholic style. Luke Miller, the one-time vicar of St. Mary the Virgin, Tottenham, then archdeacon of Hampstead, and in 2016, archdeacon of London, shared some evangelism approaches that he found useful as an Anglo-Catholic.

First it's important to recognize the great gift of a formal, involved, participatory liturgy. An Anglo-Catholic mass is very easy to involve children as acolytes and servers: This gives young people an opportunity to be engaged, and it provides an opportunity for the priest to do some teaching. Likewise, choirs can involve both children and adults, providing another chance for members of the congregation to be involved in a fairly deep way with the worship service and the substance of the faith. Luke tells of one vicar who is particularly musical and directs his own children's choir and adult choir. The vicar welcomes and encourages those who are un-catechized or otherwise newcomers to participate in the choir. In presenting the music to the choirs, he has an opportunity to explain the lyrics and do a bit of teaching about the faith. He has seen what Luke calls an "upwards spiral" toward faith through these engagements.

Anglo-Catholics often view community ministry and pastoral care as central to the work of the church. If this is seen as the task of only the priest, it can be very limiting, since one person can maintain these sorts of relationships with only a certain number of people. Still, funerals, marriages, and baptisms, when done well, can be valuable opportunities not only to serve the community but also to make connections. One clergyperson reports that nearly every funeral she has presided at has brought a new family into the church. Likewise, as we saw with St. Mary's response to the local riots, a church's response to community-wide crises is key to being seen as a vital and meaningful presence in the neighborhood.

Finally, a church can reach out to the surrounding community through a series of well-planned and well-executed programs that are meant to build upon each other. Luke calls this approach "tumbling," the way that a person can move from one program to another fairly effortlessly, making it easier to find a way into the church. Music can be a wonderful "tumbling" opportunity. Start a musical series in September, with a selection of entirely secular music performed at a high quality. In many parts of London, a considerable number of people may attend such a concert. At the concert, advertise your next event to take place in October, which will have some religious music, perhaps with some explanatory narrative (to set out some of the significance of the lyrics). The following concert will be in November, a liturgical performance of a Mozart Mass setting. People will appreciate this music, and it may draw them over the threshold, as it naturally provides some opportunity for gentle teaching. Over the course of three well-performed, free concerts, you've moved people from being concertgoers to worshipers. As Luke says, "If it's all done nicely without too much fuss on the one hand, or done sloppily on the other, many people will engage with that."

Another way to do this is with children's work. You can start with Christmas. It is fairly easy, even in London, to get people to come to a children's carol service at church, or a Christingle service.[64] Make such a service a big focal point for your work, with personal invitations, advertisements, and so forth. This sort of a service could easily draw around 150 children or so. At that service, plan to do something that will connect back with a service on or around Christmas. For example, you might have the children write a Christmas card to Jesus, which will then be presented in church on Christmas morning. This will then bring in "pester power," as children will want to return and see their Christmas card incorporated into the service.

At the Christmas service, advertise a Christingle service, which can be done around Epiphany as well as at Advent or Christmas. You might also advertise a special service for Candlemas, the Feast of the Presentation, in early February. Before people know it, they might find themselves in church three to four times in the span of two and a half months, and the children are becoming interested and invested. Coming to church doesn't seem to be such a strange thing for the family if they've been away awhile. At Candlemas, you announce a special children's activity day around Ash Wednesday. And at each event, you make announcements about the fantastic Sunday School or the youth group or Messy Church.[65] Each of these events builds on one another and draws people in a natural, nonthreatening, friendly way to become a part of the church.

A third approach is through the work of guilds: small devotional groups, perhaps focused on praying the rosary, or that make a pilgrimage to somewhere like Walsingham.[66] The shared experience of a pilgrimage in particular can be very formative for a group; they also are wonderful opportunities to invite friends and neighbors. A group could rent a bus and take a day trip, perhaps meeting with several Anglo-Catholic churches for a day of worship and devotional activities as well as free time. In his ministry at St. Mary's, Luke found these sorts of events were very popular, with guild members naturally bringing along their family and friends.

One final element in evangelism for the catholic tradition is simply confidence: to trust that the liturgy, the sacraments, scripture, common prayer, and solemn music have the power to be transformative, to lead to a genuine encounter with Christ. It can be easy to be shy and retiring about such things or retreat to claims that they just represent "our personal taste." But the catholic strand of Anglicanism has always been its most energetic and vibrant when it has seen in its worship and life not simply a personal preference or style but also a vision for all people—and all of life. As Luke says, when we have that confidence, then we can trust and "let Jesus be free to do his mission."

Conclusion

Through these stories of thriving Anglo-Catholic churches in London, we can see that growing, vital churches can be found with more formal and elaborate liturgies: Growth is not the sole preserve of charismatics and evangelicals. But as with the charismatic churches, this growth is not an accidental matter but rather comes from intentional commitment to connect with others. Churches that are growing and energized reach out to people in creative, attractive, kind, and practical ways.

Chapter 7
Lowering Thresholds: Attractional Ministries

In many parts of the Anglican Communion, the terms "church" and "parish" are synonyms; in England they are not. The parish is a geographic and demographic term: this group of people in this place. The church consists of all who attend in, participate in, and are members of the church itself. In practice, church and parish are never synonymous in England, because there is no parish where everyone is a committed churchgoer. In some parishes, the percentage of those connected with the church is very small indeed. A parish might contain Muslims, Hindus, Jews, atheists, "nones," and many others besides Christians.

Historically, residing in a parish meant the church of that parish might have a claim of some sort on you. This was especially the case before 1828, when holding political office, joining a trade guild, or operating a business required, among other things, receiving communion in the Church of England. This sort of role was a part of England's heritage of an established church. Although the church is still established by law, these obligations are no longer in operation.

Yet the parish system makes a good deal of sense for the church, in that it delineates a clear people and place to whom the church is called. These are the people the church is to serve, whether poor or well-heeled, educated or not, of whatever ethnicity or religion. In a sense, the parish is each church's mission field. It is in accepting these people where they are that one is most likely to make connections and form relationships with them.

In the past, a good deal of this connection occurred when parishioners came to the church, whether for marriage or baptism or a funeral. These occasions were seen as opportunities for gentle evangelism, for presenting the church's faith in the process of helping to serve whoever came to the church for help. In England generally, and in London in particular, fewer people are coming to the church for these traditional services.

This means the church must find other ways of making connections with their parishioners. In London, they have. These connections come through wise use of their physical plant; creative programs and intriguing engagements; commerce; music; community groups, youth centers; and groups for parents with small children. Taking the parish as the place to which it is (primarily) called, the church in London has worked to respond to the needs and opportunities right in front of it.

Opening buildings and churchyards

The Diocese of London is committed to opening its churches to the communities.[67] One of the unmissable physical features of churches in London, compared with the surrounding neighborhoods, is that they (generally) have a bit of open space around them. Particularly near the denser, expensive center of London, this space is a real luxury. Of course, historically, these spaces have been cemeteries for the church, and this is often the case today. But many churches are reordering this green space to be a gift for the community. Likewise, many churches are working to open their church buildings during the week to all and sundry who might want to visit. We have already seen this in the story of St. Michael's, Camden Town, but they are not alone.

Take St. James's, Piccadilly. An historic church just off of Piccadilly Circus, at what is for many tourists the heart of London, St. James's sits in a wide churchyard between Piccadilly and Jermyn streets, not far from the private and exclusive St. James's Square. The churchyard is kept open during the week and is home to the Piccadilly Market, available Monday to Saturday, featuring on Mondays a food market, Tuesdays an antiques and collectibles market, and other days a range of arts and crafts. Their churchyard also includes The Southwood Garden, which was refurbished in 2012 and offers quiet and rest in a green, well-tended garden. The Caravan, a drop-in counseling service, is also found in the churchyard (located in a caravan, fittingly), serving people in that location since 1982.

St. James's also keeps its doors open during the week, and many take the opportunity to enter. Some come in to sleep, others to pray or meditate in the quiet, and yet others to enjoy the restored Christopher Wren structure, to see where William Blake was baptized, or to ponder the occasional art installations. St. James's does a good job in keeping its church building open and hospitable to many different people.

St. James's also regularly features artistic engagements with public issues from the perspective of Christian faith. For example, in 2013 they staged what they called Bethlehem Unwrapped. Taking the place of the usual Christmas market in their churchyard, Bethlehem Unwrapped featured the erecting of an eight-meter wall across the front of the church, prominently visible from the street. The idea was to push beyond the usual Victorian ideas of Christmas and to dramatize the reality of the city of Bethlehem, where Jesus was born. The wall was installed in place from December 23 to January 5. During these weeks, St. James's held a festival in the churchyard with events including a poetry slam, a film showing, an evening of stand-up comedy, a feast catered by Israeli chef Yotam Ottolenghi and Palestinian chef Sami Tamimi, a concert, and much more. They encouraged visitors to interact with the wall and to write on it messages of peace and support for those who live behind the wall. Over the two weeks, roughly 2,000 people a day visited. Print and online media from across the world featured stories on the installation.[68] Since then, St. James's has featured thought-provoking art installations related to global climate change and the Syrian refugee crisis.

St. James's is near the center of London with a great deal of foot traffic every day. Other churches farther from the city center also work to open their buildings and offer their churchyards as assets to the local community. St. Paul's, West Hackney, for example, possesses a very large and green churchyard in an area that had few open spaces. Yet its grounds sat behind locked gates, unused and overgrown. The people of St. Paul's and their rector, Niall Weir, spearheaded an effort along with local residents to rehabilitate and reopen the area to the community. They received a grant from the Heritage Lottery Fund to redevelop the site, including a recreation ground for more active uses, a more naturally developed area around the church's burial ground, and a newly refinished forecourt for the church site.[69] This last area is home to a popular Saturday farmers' market, operated by Growing Communities, which brings in around 1,000 people each week.

Growing Communities also makes use of a portion of St. Paul's ground as part of their organic "patchwork farm" located at various sites in Hackney and Dagenham. The produce is sold at the farmers' market and as part of a community-supported agriculture produce box program. In addition, Growing Communities uses their patch at St. Paul's to train people in growing organic produce. St. Paul's church hall is also in near-constant use by the church and local charities to assist the homeless, those with various addictions, people involved in the sex trade, the unemployed, and the young. Although St. Paul's does not report marked growth in attendance at worship, it is a vital and vibrant Christian community, connecting with numerous sorts of people, in a neighborhood with a sizable and growing Turkish Muslim population.

Not far east of St. Paul's lies the church of St. John at Hackney, which we heard about in chapter three. They also rethought and redeveloped their church site, doing so with the help of the local council. Likewise sensing a lack of open space in the neighborhood, the church cleared a graveyard to make space for a farmers' market, children's play area, refreshment stand, public lavatories, community garden, and open green space.

Beyond that, the congregation has opened up the church structure itself as a venue for events. Reordering their worship space, removing pews and replacing them with flexible seating, has been essential for this. They have since hosted concerts with musicians such as Coldplay, Elbow, and Emily Sandborn. Rob Wickham, rector of St. John's at the time reckons that in 2012 alone, somewhere around 40,000 people crossed the threshold into the church for these concerts. The church also hosts the Hackney Children's Theatre, which puts on shows for children. In three years, Wickham reports, they presented fifteen performances, which brought around 5,000 people through the doors of St. John's. Alongside these creative shows, the church hosted a job fair before the London Olympics in

2012, which attracted more than 500 teenagers to interview for living wage jobs in the Olympic Park during the games. He credits a measure of St. John's growth in attendance at worship to these events, which get "people inside the building, and they see that it isn't a scary mausoleum but actually quite a vibrant space." From 2007 to 2014, average Sunday attendance grew from seventy-six to around 180: these numbers also reflect the beginning of two new services. Beyond numbers at Sunday services, attendance at occasional service such as the children's carol service at Christmas has grown, from seventy in 2007 to around 600 six years later.

Other churches are more focused and modest in the ways they open their churches to the neighborhood. St. Mary's in Islington worked intentionally and carefully to open their building to people during the week. Given what was already available in the area—they sit next to a restaurant, for example—they decided that they were not called to something like opening a café. What was in short supply was an area just to sit in quiet, for free: everywhere else required at least the cost of a cup of coffee. They chose to open their church for people to rest, meditate, or pray. At first, they only opened it a few hours a week, when it could be staffed by a volunteer supervisor. But after some prayerful consideration and consulting with advisors, they decided to stop using volunteers and simply open the church building in the morning and close it around 4 p.m. Although they rented out the space in the church basement for events, they chose not to do so with the church, allowing it to retain its focus as a place for connection with God.[70] St. Mary's estimates that perhaps thirty people a day cross over the threshold. Although these numbers may not compare with St. John's, St. Mary's has nevertheless seen some growth in attendance: During the first year of intentionally keeping their facility open to the public at worship, they saw an increase of about 17 percent in worship and an impressive 48 percent rise in the number of children attending worship.[71]

This effort has brought other fruit as well: As Simon Harvey, vicar of St. Mary's puts it, "for the church community it's broken the myth that the world outside is hostile to the church….Once you've made a decision that your job is to keep people out, then everything else follows from that. It'll come through in everything—probably the preaching too! But the opposite's equally true. We've become much more confident and relaxed as a church since we started opening it."[72]

Helping people wherever they find themselves

Another way that churches in London successfully lower the threshold to bring people in is by offering practical courses to help people in their day-to-day lives. This goes beyond classes that introduce the faith such as Alpha.

Holy Trinity Brompton (HTB) began one such program called The Money Course. It offers practical advice on money management, informed by Christian teaching (although it is very specifically intended to be accessible to anyone, of any faith or none). The eight-session course aims to help people gain control over their money through making prudent decisions about its use and getting in the habit of creating and living by a budget. The format of the course is similar to Alpha: People arrive and have time to socialize together over a meal. A large group talk is given, whether live or pre-recorded. Then people break up into small groups to discuss the issues raised in the talk, whether people's relationship to money, budgeting, setting financial goals, saving, or reducing debt. Sessions with a one-to-one budget coach are also available. For those who come to the course in need of debt relief, they are able to provide some debt counseling through a charity called Crosslight Advice that offers free and confidential help with debt.[73] The course provides help to people regardless of their faith or background, while also bringing them into a church building for a meeting and providing some indirect and gentle witness to them about the Christian faith. Whether people respond in faith or not, they are blessed with some genuine skills and knowledge with which to help themselves.

St. Paul's, Hammersmith, early on sensed that God was calling them to set down roots in the neighborhood. Although they were planted by HTB, which tends to attract people from across the city, they don't aim to be a gathered church in the same way. They work to have a more localized presence. All of the church's activities that are "sponsored from the center" (that receive time and attention in announcements, newsletters, e-mail, website, and so forth) are Hammersmith-based.

Noticing that disadvantaged young people in the area were having trouble moving into full-time work (and thereby being left out of society in a number of ways), they decided to found a charity called Resurgo. This charity in turn devised a program called Spear, dedicated to building bridges between young people (ages sixteen to twenty-four) and employers. For young people, Spear offers a six-week program that teaches the skills needed to find and retain meaningful employment. The organization also has a team of recruiters who work with businesses to develop an institutional culture in which entry-level workers can grow and flourish; this involves training managers to work effectively as coaches for young people entering the work force as well as providing job placement for graduates of the Spear program. Spear has become a trusted, go-to source for new employees and has helped more than 5,000 young people find work over the last decade—and today, nine centers for Spear programs are offered around London.

Spear does not have an explicit witness to Christian faith (in part because it would restrict funding for the program). But St.

Paul's considers this work intrinsic to its mission. As Will Leaf, associate vicar at St. Paul's puts it, although people coming to relationship with Jesus is important to St. Paul's, "we're willing to sponsor this kind of work even if we never talk to anyone about Jesus because we're demonstrating by our actions that these people have value, that they don't need to be victims. And so we're seeing people set free, which is what Jesus does." As he expresses it, both evangelism and social transformation are part of the missional DNA of St. Paul's.

Witness through music

We've seen how churches lower thresholds through transforming their facilities and grounds and by offering practical courses to their communities. Another group of churches are lowering thresholds for people to enter in by offering more usual activities such as music programs and worship services, although with creative twists.

When you think of high-quality music and London churches, you might especially think of St. Martin-in-the-Fields on Trafalgar Square. Many Americans in particular know this church's name through the recordings of The Academy of St. Martin in the Fields, a chamber orchestra founded there in 1959. It remains well-known for music, featuring regular lunchtime and evening concerts. On these occasions, the church's body is often filled with listeners, many drawn from around the world and passing through Trafalgar Square as tourists. In an average year, somewhere between 400 and 500 concerts, choral recitals, or other professional musical events find a home in St. Martin's.

When Sam Wells became vicar of St. Martin's in 2012, he saw that the church was filled for lunchtime concerts four out of five days of the week. The remaining day, Thursday, was quite notably empty; on this day the church held a regularly scheduled lunchtime eucharist. Perhaps twenty people came. Wells tried one thing and then another, with no change in attendance. Finally, instead of continuing to fight against and resist the lure of concerts, he decided to work with it.

Bringing in the St. Martin's Voices choir and musicians, Wells created a program entitled Great Sacred Music presented every Thursday at 1 p.m. This thirty-five-minute sequence of choral works intends "to speak to heart, head, and soul," as the tagline puts it. Interwoven among these pieces is Wells himself, who introduces the works with historical, musicological, and—crucially—theological background for the listeners. Choral works might be chosen thematically: the Trinity, around Trinity Sunday, or an abbreviated service of lessons and carols near Christmas. Sometimes they are arranged by composer, either contemporary or historical: selections from Mozart's Requiem, for example, or from contemporary British composer Cecilia McDowall. Other times, the selections coalesce around an event in the world: music to mark the 100th anniversary of the Battle of the Somme, for example.

The program is free and well attended. Where before Wells struggled to have twenty at Eucharist, now upwards of 250 people from around the world flock to the church at lunchtime on Thursdays to hear Wells set forth the Christian faith, in the context of beautiful and sophisticated choral music.

Children and parents: Messy Church

St. Nicholas' Church, in London's East End, has worked hard to make connections with its neighborhood by lowering thresholds. The church has an unconventional story. Built in the early 1950s, the style of the building is typically postwar modern, but it has an elaborate mural on its ceiling. Following a period of decline, the church closed in 1969 and then served as a warehouse for vinyl LP records for several decades. In 1998, it reopened for worship thanks to the efforts of All Saints', Poplar, in whose parish the church stands. The church was formally rededicated in 2000, and the church and hall have been refurbished.

Jane Hodges serves as the team rector for the parish, which includes both St. Nicholas and All Saints churches. About forty worship at St. Nicholas on a Sunday; growth has been slow and organic, through building relationships in the area. This is due in part to Jane and her family living close to the church and being willing to strike up conversations with people on the sidewalks. Also key was hiring a staff member to work with families and children, who lived in the area beforehand and knows it well. Living locally is important, the two explain, as it means that they are present at the school gates at pick up and drop off, along with the other parents. If there is a stabbing in the street, the leaders are affected by it as much as the members of the church and their neighbors. Jane wears her collar regularly as she walks through the parish so that people know who she is, that they can come up and talk to her, and that she might come up and talk with them.

The church is situated on the Aberfeldy Estate in an area with a high percentage of what in America we call public housing. About 80 percent of the mostly poorer community is ethnically Bengali and Muslim. Unlike many other areas of London, families tend to remain in the neighborhood for generations. Many in the area are quite vulnerable and often lead hard lives. Many larger, extended families live in the community.

Given this context, St. Nicholas has begun a number of specialized programs for the area. First, on Friday mornings at 10 a.m., they have what they call Buggy Mass. This is a service of eucharist devised specifically for parents or other caregivers with young children—they often come with their baby buggies, parking them at the back of the nave. The service features a number of child-appropriate songs, Bible readings, a brief sermon, and a craft response time. Children are welcome to sit on the floor, in the middle of the moveable seating. Communion is offered with reverence and flexibility. Parents, leaders, and children then gather for tea, coffee, juice, and cookies in a side room following the service. The service provides an opportunity for parents to meet other parents, for children to socialize and learn the faith from an early age, and for all to worship God.

Messy Church is a program that has spread worldwide. It began simply, with one church's frustration with its inability to connect with children and their families. It is a Christ-centered program intended to engage children as children, with creativity, hospitality, and celebration. It generally meets on an afternoon and features a time of creative interaction with a Bible story, a celebration that typically includes story, prayer, song, or games, and a sit-down meal together. It is intended to be a church service in itself, not an additional meeting, and is meant especially for those who are not already involved in a church. All elements of the service aim to be for all ages, not only children. It is a simple and flexible structure that can be adapted to individual communities. Since it is meant as a standalone church service, beginning a Messy Church is actually, for all intents and purposes, planting a new congregation. In fact, around 40 percent of new church growth across England as a whole is owed to Messy Church, according to Ric Thorpe.

Jane and her team have worked to bring Messy Church to St. Nicholas. Although they enjoyed some initial success, they also found that it can be labor intensive and takes a large group of dedicated volunteers, which was sometimes difficult for their members. Other places run a Messy Church program monthly: They meet to discuss and plan for two weeks in advance to bring it all together, then hold the service, and then take two weeks to rest. But given the shape of peoples' lives in the parish, they found it difficult to prepare in this way. It was often hard to find twelve to fifteen volunteers. People were eager to help, but they couldn't commit to being involved in the weeks-long planning; typically, they could only show up on the day Messy Church was held. So they adapted their process and now carry out the bulk of the behind-the-scenes preparation work themselves. This means volunteers can show up on the day of the service and be given jobs and roles that are ready to go. It also means that, owing to the amount of preparation involved, rather than having monthly Messy Church, they offer the service four or five times a year, with a theme such as Messy Harvest, Messy Christmas, Messy Easter, and Messy Pentecost. Jane makes sure, whenever possible, to display some of the craft items made in Messy Church for the services later in the week, to connect this service with the rest of the life of the church. Messy Church struggled for a few years, but Jane now reports that it has taken off and is thriving.

Although it has been a messy process learning how best to run Messy Church at St. Nicholas', they have experienced a good response to the program, with around eighty people attending, including about four or five Muslim families who come regularly—a few of whom have also come to worship at the church.

Adapting to the surrounding community

Some churches have reconfigured their entire lives around the life of their parish. For example, take St. Mary Woolnoth and St. Margaret Lothbury, both located in the City of London, the city center area that features a dense collection of churches remaining from ancient London and now surrounded by offices and very few residences. St. Mary's building was designed by Nicholas Hawksmoor and is situated above Bank Underground Station; St. Margaret's dates from the twelfth century and was redesigned by the office of Christopher Wren following the great fire in the seventeenth century. Today, the churches focus their ministry on lunchtime services of informal worship and teaching. They explicitly advertise these as being open to "come and go as you wish" so that employees can return to work when necessary. Lunchtime organ recitals are also common. Services are planned with this in mind. They also feature a thirty-minute Tuesday lunchtime communion service. The church buildings are open from early in the mornings until just past 5 p.m. during the week for prayer or quiet reflection. They offer before-work and after-work prayer meetings, men's and women's group breakfasts, and small-group meetings. Because of the nature of their neighborhood, neither church does any work with children nor, indeed, does either of them hold any Sunday services.

Conclusion

Through all of these stories, we have seen how the church in London is lowering thresholds to invite people in: through opening their doors and churchyards and through the use of art, music, practical courses for life, and innovative worship services. This has resulted in faithful and creative ministry as the churches connect with the community. Sometimes, these initiatives have resulted in numerical growth, occasionally even dramatic growth. Sometimes it has not. But the churches do this not for the sake of numbers but in order to serve and expand God's kingdom.

Chapter 8

Crossing Thresholds: The Church Taking Shape Among Our Neighbors

If some churches have worked to lower their thresholds so that it is easier for people to enter, others have chosen to cross their thresholds into the neighborhood to meet people where they are—in some cases, leaving behind their buildings altogether.

Most of these endeavors might be called Fresh Expressions of Church.[74] Fresh Expressions is a movement that began in England in the early twenty-first century and includes many different kinds of Christians. This movement seeks to transform people and communities and make new disciples through encouraging various ways of being church in the world. It exists alongside the traditional church (rather than seeking to replace it), in what former Archbishop Rowan Williams called a "mixed economy" of church.[75] A few of these are former traditional churches, but most are new ministry startups.

Fresh Expressions of Church doesn't start with a fixed model of how the church ought to look: church building, parking lot, governing board, pews, Sunday worship.[76] Instead, they begin with the people that they intend to reach, people who are not already a part of the local church. This means that the forms of fresh expressions are as various as the people who are engaged: There is no one model that needs to be copied. There is a fresh expression that works with surfers, another that consists of people learning English, others that are made up of East Asian immigrants, parents with children, or retirees. Others might look a bit more traditional but meet in unusual places, such as a café or pub. Some are neighborhood-based, some are focused on housing developments, and others work with schools or community centers. The key to them all is context: Who's here? What is their life like? What might faith in Jesus look like for them?

It's important, too, that fresh expressions of church are not begun by or sustained by individuals. Deep in the DNA of the movement is the idea that small groups of people are needed to support and encourage one another, to listen together, to serve together. Most of those who start fresh expressions are laypeople—around 70 percent—rather than ordained clergy.

Although the forms of fresh expressions vary widely, folks tend to follow a general "journey." There are several elements of this journey, but these are not strict "stages." They often tend to be messy and not strictly linear.

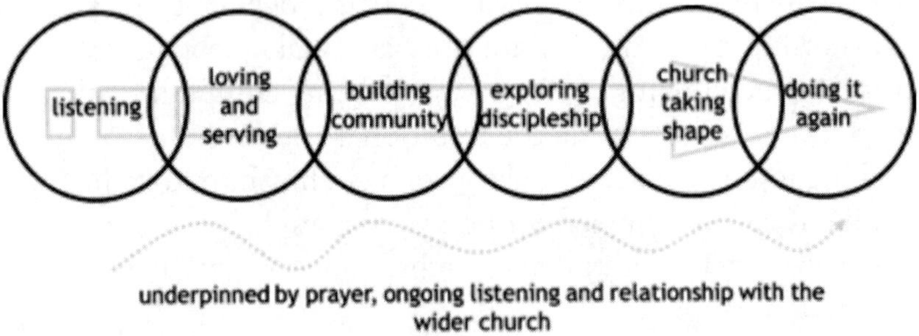

A fresh expression of church begins with **listening** and with working to set aside prior assumptions about what is needed or wanted in a particular setting. We might be tempted to think we know the answers before we even begin listening to the questions people are actually asking. But fresh expressions begin with deep listening and working to clear away what we think we already know people need.

This is done in order to **love and serve** people where they are. This could be a matter of bringing in pastries and fresh fruit and making good quality coffee for an office setting where people feel isolated. It might be throwing a weekend barbecue for an apartment complex where you live in which people don't seem to know each other. Perhaps it is starting an English as a second language course for spouses of international students at the local university. Maybe a nearby block is vacant and blighted, and people from the neighborhood could be brought together to plant a community garden. It might be a couple of Christians who restore classic cars wanting to connect with others in the classic car community. Maybe a population of recent college graduates could use some guidance on finances. The possibilities are as particular and varied as the settings we find ourselves in. It also may not be obvious what the best form of loving and serving might be and may involve trial and error for a time.

These acts of loving service provide opportunities to get to know people, to form relationships and even friendships. This is the step of **building community.** The forms this community takes are as different as the groups: perhaps it is a moms and toddlers gathering, a clutch of local gardeners, or a group of homeless people. Building community is valuable in itself: Providing a setting in which people can know others and be known, have a sense of belonging, and share who they are, is a great good—and rare enough these days. This is a significant gift the fresh expressions team offers.

Within community, opportunities come up naturally for team members to share their faith. If someone becomes interested, they are invited—perhaps along with their family or friends—

to meet and chat. This can become the basis for a friendly, non-threatening small group to investigate Jesus and the Christian faith. You can use materials from Alpha, Emmaus, or another course or resources provided by your church—or create your own, exploring one of the gospels, for example. Or you can invite an individual to join with the fresh expressions leadership team, which meets weekly for Bible study and prayer. In some cases, the community itself might function as a small group. For instance, you might build community with a group focused on images of new life in film or discussion of news stories from a moral or spiritual angle. The key is a genuine invitation to come and see who this Jesus is and what it means to follow him. This is the step of **exploring discipleship**.

I've set out here three different ways through the journey: One forms a separate group to explore discipleship, one brings inquirers into a preexisting group with the leadership team, and one sees the entire fresh expression effort as a group. Determining the strategy that is best for you depends on whom you're connecting with and serving.[77]

Many elements of what we might call "holistic evangelism" help move the journey along. These range from acts of kindness to talking about the significance of faith to you to a simple act of worship, an experience of healing, or any number of other acts of love that connect with another person. Exploring discipleship should not be a surprise, as if it were a bait-and-switch tactic. It should be clear from the beginning that this little group of people is Christian and is motivated by their faith.

And as the group starts out with the fresh expression, it should also have a sense for where people in the community are in relation to the church and Christian faith. Are people hostile or suspicious of Christians and the church? Your task might be earning trust or showing vulnerability, alongside deep listening. Are people complacent? How can their appetites be stoked to learn more about Jesus? Are people on the cusp of faith? How can they be encouraged to turn to Jesus and to grow deeply and authentically?

In some settings, you may find that many who are part of the developing community are already practicing Christians. The primary goal of Fresh Expressions of Church is bringing faith in Jesus in new ways to people and places where it is not already present, and so there is no desire to "poach" folks from existing churches. But you may encounter some people who are intrigued and excited by what the team is doing and want to join and support the fresh expression in their spare time, alongside their participation in their local church.

Of course, many may not show interest, and that's okay. These acts of service and forming community are a part of God's kingdom coming. They are significant and meaningful on their own. If they went no further than this, if in God's wisdom this seemed as far as the team could go, then it would not be a failure. But this is not the full journey of Fresh Expressions.

As a small group gathers or the leadership team welcomes newcomers, the group explores the Christian faith together. Some may come to faith. Gradually, a group forms that can begin considering what being the church in their context might look like. This is the stage of **church taking shape.** The group needs to consider, over time, what mission, worship, pastoral care, and relations with the larger church will look like. Or as one person put it, the group will explore "what's involved in growing UP toward Christ, OUT in service to others, IN deepening fellowship, and being part OF the body of Christ."[78] This conversation happens in the space between the local culture and context and the Christian faith and tradition.

It's important to understand that this is not a matter of bringing a "prefabricated" church to this new community. As people move into faith, they're not then handed the inherited church: If that had been meaningful for them, they would have presumably already been a part of it. Instead, the group works to express its Christian faith in ways that are authentic to itself. Acts of worship might be very simple or brief rather than using an extensive liturgy. Rather than three scripture lessons and a psalm, as in many typical Episcopal or Lutheran services, one brief lesson might be used. They might not keep the seasons of the church year or celebrate the eucharist or have any ordained leaders.

Instead of a sermon, a response time might look like a discovery Bible study. This takes a chunk of the Bible, most often from one of the gospels, and asks questions like: *If this story happened today, what would it look like? What does this story mean to me? Could this story make a difference to my life?* After some time away, the group might return to the story and ask: *Did the story make a difference to my life?*

All of this requires some trust on the part of those who initiated the fresh expression, as they are not in complete control of the process! But it is appropriate that they be a part of the process. At this stage, as the church takes shape, they can have important input. For example, there might be a time when one of the more seasoned leaders suggests "in the church, we have a time where we confess our sins to God and receive God's forgiveness." The leader explains why and how it's done in the church and then asks if (and how) this group might do something similar. Together, they might devise some new form for this or decide to try out a traditional form for a while to see how it goes. This allows the group to move more deeply into faith and worship while also expressing confession (or another practice) in ways authentic to itself.

Finally, a flourishing fresh expression of church shows signs of life and growth. This growth is not expected to be huge: Fresh expressions is not a formula for a megachurch but a framework for small, new Christian communities in mission, connecting with new people in new ways. The growth will be less in terms of becoming one large community and more along the lines of reproducing other small communities living in mission. This is the stage of **do it again.** A community that begins in mission is not aiming to become settled or inward-looking but to continue living out its calling.

St. Luke in the High Street

One example of Fresh Expressions of Church was undertaken by an entire congregation. St. Luke's Church, Walthamstow, had at one point been a thriving congregation, touched profoundly by charismatic renewal, but this energy dissipated by the early 2000s. The congregation was aging and fading, with an expensive facility to maintain. Faced with what seemed an overwhelming and unsustainable situation, they set about to pray and discern what God was calling them to.

Around 2007, they realized their building was not much of an asset. Tucked back in the middle of a residential neighborhood, it was effectively invisible. On top of that, they had a growing sense that they were called to be out with people, where they were. They weren't supposed to be an exclusive destination, hidden away and accessible only to those "in the know." In short, they were called to be out on Main Street—or as they know it in Britain—the High Street.

They decided to move out of their church building and to join with the Walthamstow Farmers' Market, which is set up in a prominent place in the High Street every Sunday from 10 a.m. to 2 p.m. The team vicar of St. Luke's also serves as manager for the market, supporting the vendors and overseeing set-up and take-down each Sunday. Members of St. Luke's run a stall of their own where they provide tea, coffee, and cakes and are available for anyone who would like to have a chat or pray. They are present with people where they are, listening, loving, and serving; they also hope that this can be a forum in which people can be invited into other places to further explore faith. They're now known as St. Luke's in the High Street.

The Sunday morning farmers' market is not the only activity of the church. They also gather at other times during the month in members' homes for worship (on a Wednesday evening for what they call "More Worship"), for fellowship, sharing meals at "Second Breakfast" (on the second Saturday of the month) and "Last Supper" (on the last Wednesday of the month), and at other times for Bible study. The church also features "Time Team," a group of eight lay volunteers, responsible along with the vicar for running the church's activities and providing pastoral care.[79]

Frances Shoesmith serves as the current team vicar for St. Luke's. She tells about the way St. Luke's responded to an opportunity. They had noticed that the farmers' market stall had begun attracting people from around the margins of society, some with mental health problems, long-term unemployment, or addictions. These folks appreciated the free hot drinks but were also sometimes hungry. St. Luke's had begun meeting in a local café run by a Turkish Muslim for Breakfast, Bible, and Chat. They invited some of these more vulnerable folks to join them, and the group quickly swelled to as many as twenty-five. St. Luke's buys breakfast (from a pre-selected list of options) for those who cannot pay, and they gather in groups of four around tables to explore a passage of the Bible. The passages are short, from a simplified English version of the Bible, and questions are pitched at an introductory level, which allows a wide variety of people from many different backgrounds to join in, whether Christian, non-Christian, unchurched, or de-churched.

The nature of these sorts of ministries is that they are often only for a season, or constantly changing. The Breakfast, Bible, and Chat group has gone through a number of iterations. At one point, they realized that a number of people were taking advantage of the free breakfast but unwilling to engage the group, so they changed from a full breakfast to tea and toast. As a result, they lost several folks. On top of that, the café where they had met for several years closed, and so they had to find another location. But this is the nature of such ministry, often changing with the ebb and flow of life rather than fixed and established for generations.

They are also making a transition to being a lay-led ministry that is part of the parish team ministry.[80] This is not an unrealistic way forward for them, since the lay members of the church are used to leading groups, working with the farmers' market, chatting with strangers over tea or coffee, and working with the population of vulnerable people in the area.

For those accustomed to a settled church service in a traditional church structure with a typical clergy person, St. Luke's in the High Street might feel very odd, even foreign. But for those who are a part of this ministry, it feels quite natural, the fruit of following God's call out into the High Street.

The Deeper Network Church

The Deeper Network Church is another fresh expression. Founded by a group of younger adults from an established church in eastern London, they sought to discern where God was calling them. They prayed, they discussed, they looked around them—and they realized that something like 10-12,000 young adults come into the central Romford neighborhood every weekend to go to the pubs and clubs. Wanting to reach these people with the love of Jesus, they realized they needed to go out and be present with them in order to connect with them.

So in 2009 they began setting up a "Deeper Lounge" booth on Friday nights near the pubs and clubs. They offer free soft drinks from 10 p.m. until 2 a.m. They're there to chat and get to know people where they're at, people they reckon aren't otherwise engaged by the church and would never think to be a part of a church. They serve alongside a number of street pastors, working together to look out for and connect with the people there.

In 2013, the group began to rent out a retail space in the nearby business district of central Romford. They use it for worship, meeting space for youth work, and a community café. The Deeper Network Church meets as a whole community twice a month; otherwise, the church consists as a collection of Missional Communities (MCs).

Missional Communities

Missional Communities are another approach to Fresh Expressions. One author describes them in this way:

> [Missional Communities] are a way of living the Christian life communally in ordinary homes through supernatural power. They are the way redeemed people live locally; the organic way disciples follow Jesus together in everyday life. They emerge when truly converted people stop living their own lives for their own ends and begin living a community life according to the values of the Kingdom of God, sharing their lives and resources with those Christians and not-yet-Christians around them.[81]

Annie Kirke, who served for a time as pioneer for missional communities in the Diocese of London says that they are "a potent mix of the relational, spontaneous, and organic, mixed with an intentionality to grow the kingdom where we live."

Missional Communities tend to carry out their work in five ways. But at the heart of each is a small group of people intentionally living out the gospel in a community.

A Missional Community may be a household, whether a family or group of friends, who are committed to God's mission in a particular area or group of people. They live as disciples of Jesus, living out generous hospitality and relational evangelism. Often, these households embrace one of the other forms of missional community as well.

A second form of a Missional Community is a simple church. These groups of ten to twenty people focus on living a common life in Christ and sharing the good news of Jesus. With an emphasis on face-to-face relationships, groups meet regularly in a home, common room of an apartment complex, café, pub, or other third space. They feature common meals, simple Bible studies, and everyday spiritual disciplines. A simple church doesn't seek to grow into a larger church but to birth other simple churches.

A Missional Community might also choose to become a discipleship movement, in which the group focuses on intentionally sharing the good news of Jesus with others. This involves prayer, relationship-building, seeking out what are known as "people of peace"[82] and engaging activities such as discovery Bible studies (outlined earlier).

Some Missional Communities pursue entrepreneurial projects. These groups choose to begin a project together. This might be a social entrepreneurship opportunity, such as starting a cleaning company that pays a living wage or uses ex-offenders to provide work experience after prison. It might be opening a café, laundromat, or childcare facility in an underserved area. It might be some other kind of business or creative project. But behind the project is a group of people committed to supporting each other and living intentionally for the kingdom of God.

A final form of Missional Community is a network community. These groups focus on living out the good news of Jesus in connection with a particular shared interest, vocation, or other activity: a sports team, a hobby such as restoring classic cars or knitting, a pastime such as fishing, gardening, cooking, or bicycling, or people engaged in a particular vocation such as law enforcement or accountancy. Groups might also be comprised of folks in one kind of recovery or another: overeating or alcoholism, for example.

In London, Mark Bishop and Phil Hoyle are priests whose calls include leading missional communities. Mark leads a community based in Vale Estate, a 1950s housing project. Phil heads up a Missional Community located just east of Acton Vale, in Shepherd's Bush, which is focused on artists and others in the creative industries.

But as with Fresh Expressions, there is no particular reason why a Missional Community needs an ordained leader. What they do need are people dedicated to living out their faith in Christ publicly, with integrity, and animated to love, serve, and connect with others who are not like them.

Pioneer Ministers

A final, related vocation is that of pioneer minister, sometimes shortened to just "pioneer." If the term pioneer rankles or doesn't make sense in your context, you could also call them ministry entrepreneurs. The entire focus of those who work in this capacity—lay or ordained, individual or group—is starting something new. These pioneer ministers have the capacity to see a new and different future and are able to work now to make that future possible. The Church of England explains: "Pioneers are people called by God who are the first to see and creatively respond to the Holy Spirit's initiatives with those outside the church, gathering others around them as they seek to establish new contextual Christian community."[83]

One pioneer minister is Annie McTighe, who was called to plant a church on the former Olympic Village site in the northeast of London. Following the 2012 Olympics, the area was redeveloped as a new area of housing, with extensive retail, education, and other services. The site actually straddles the dioceses of London and Chelmsford, so this is in ways a joint effort. Her position is paid through the Church of England's Mission Development Funding. This allows the church to become proactively present to a community that in 2013, had no residents, but when development is complete, will have 40,000 homes.[84]

Since arriving in 2014, Annie has spent her time getting to know and love the residents there. She frequently hosts dinner parties in her apartment and is known not to turn down invitations to others. She has become involved with the schools and developed relationships with the police officers in the area. She works with students at the several universities that have opened campuses in the area. She has done "Ashes to Go," in which, in full vestments, she positioned herself outside the local Tube Station and offered to mark people with the traditional ash cross from Ash Wednesday, telling them "Remember you are dust, and to dust you shall return." And she has drawn together a small community in the form of Church E20, which meets on Tuesday nights in a local café for a simple dinner, prayer, and a Bible study or other program. (E20 is the postcode in which the former Olympic Village is located.) Formally instituted as the pioneer vicar for the area, Annie is clear that her primary work is relational, getting to know and care about the people who live in the community.

Chapter 9
Community Organizing and Evangelism

One final aspect of the church in London is its engagement with various kinds of community organizing and community development. We have already seen several elements of this commitment, from the church's commitment to serving a parish to churches' responses to social upheavals such as the riots in 2011. For many churches in London, community organizing is in their genes.

Very often, community organizing and evangelism go hand-in-glove. Service in and with the community is seen explicitly as a way in which Christians may live out their faith in the world as well as being a way of bearing witness to others about new life in Christ. This sharing of the good news is not heavy handed, but it is intentional. At the same time, community involvement is not seen as only a means to the end of growing the church. That would not be authentic service. What I have witnessed is that much of the church in London understands service and evangelism not as an either/or dilemma but rather as both/and. One good example of this combination is the Engine Room at Hale Village.

Hale Village is a new housing development in North London, steps away from the Tottenham Hale tube station. The new development is taking the place of a former industrial site and includes housing for university students, social housing, affordable housing, and market-rate housing. Work was begun on the site in 2008, progressing in stages over several years. Across the road from Hale Village is another, older housing development called the Ferry Lane Estate, begun in the early 1970s.

The Engine Room got its beginning in 2011. Andrew Kwapong and his wife, Martina, began by spending time in the area, meeting people on the street, going to school meetings, and getting to know community groups as well as the issues facing people in the area. They spent time with teachers, parents, students, and administrators in the nearby Ferry Lane Primary School. They started this initiative without any meeting space or infrastructure and simply dedicated themselves to meeting people where they were.

One way they began doing this was by putting together pop-up cafés. They would pay attention to where people were naturally present and when—for example, the period of time after school pick-up—and bring together tables and chairs, coffee, tea and soft drinks, and cakes and other treats. This gave them an opportunity to meet the residents and chat.

They soon found that these pop-up cafés offered opportunities for residents to meet each other. This was important in two ways. At Hale Village, many people were moving into the development with no roots in the area, no friends or acquaintances, and few opportunities to make any. Everyone was a newcomer. People came from many different backgrounds and might not normally be friendly with the folks they lived next to or across the courtyard from. Pop-up cafés and other open-air activities identified a need of building community—and offered a response.

Across the street at the Ferry Lane Estate, the community had a different need. This older development is all social housing, that is, affordable homes for those on limited incomes or receiving state benefits. People may have lived there for a generation or more. Yet because of fear, many did not know their neighbors. As one woman said to Andrew, "I've lived on this estate for years, and now I've just begun to get to know my neighbors." The pop-up cafés gave residents a safe space to get to know one another.

Andrew and Martina quickly realized that this work was not only giving them an opportunity to meet people but also serving a crucial function in the two communities as a "third place." As we discussed earlier, the first place is where you live; the second place is where you work. But the third place is somewhere where you spend time that is neither work nor home. Pubs, coffeehouses, some restaurants, public parks, and many other sites can function as "third places." Urban sociologist Ray Oldenburg argues that these places are crucial to our functioning as people and as a society: They are important for human community.[85] For different reasons, Hale Village and the Ferry Lane Estate did not have effective third places, and this was something that the Engine Room could provide. Alongside noticing this lack of dedicated third spaces, Andrew and Martina also realized that, in the busy and dynamic life of the city, a third place might be defined by time as much as place, for example, at 9:10 a.m. gathering at the bus stop after parents have dropped off children at school or as people arrive home from work and pass through an area.

Although at first Andrew and Martina focused on Hale Village, they soon sensed a call to Ferry Lane as well. They had space dedicated to their work on the grounds of Hale Village, but they also needed to find ways to be present across the street. Whereas the new residents of Hale Village had a sense of hope, coming into a new place, Andrew detected that folks at Ferry

Lane had been "burned" a number of times in the past and had less sense of hope. In response to this, Andrew made three commitments.

First, while Andrew and Martina had a new set of community rooms at Hale Village, they would work extra hard to be a visible presence at Ferry Lane, including more pop-up cafés and involvement with the school. They had been bringing in a double-decker bus to host a mobile youth club to Hale Village, which had drawn in a good number of kids but none from Ferry Lane. As a result, they moved the site for the bus across the street; as a result, residents of Ferry Lane started getting involved.

Second, they approached their work as one of building relationships, not serving as landlords. This meant that they would commit themselves to involving local people from both estates in the work of the Engine Room. This included involving people on a formal basis: For example, they hired a Ferry Lane resident to serve part-time as an administrator. Ultimately, they decided that all of the activities run through the Engine Room would be run by local residents and local organizations and charities. They saw this as an opportunity to journey with people in the area, becoming partners with them in blessing this place.

This is distinctly different than coming in as professionals with all the answers to "help" people. It encourages local residents to become involved in the transformation of their own lives. This was particularly important, Andrew said, with those who live on the Ferry Lane Estate. As in other places in the world, London has often responded to unrest or social deprivation in a top-down manner. In the wake of rioting, for example, money would be found to erect a new community center; managers and social workers would be sent in with no real connection to the neighborhood and little engagement with the surrounding area. In the end, this type of approach served not to heal the community but was simply a grand gesture by the government to show they were "doing something." And the residents in Tottenham recognized this type of "help." They come by their cynicism honestly.

Andrew and Martina have committed themselves to the idea that time and energy—relationships—are more important than money and infrastructure. Although they have a useful, accessible space in the center of Hale Village, they are also clear that they are involved with it as a church, not simply as landlords. This means that they do not rent the space to all organizations but work to partner with other groups as a means to engage the community.

Even as they have established a structure, Andrew and Martina place a premium on leaving the building and spending time on the streets. This gives them visibility in both estates and helps them to meet more people and be more engaged.

Engine Room programs are intended to serve and bless the community while also building relationships as a Christian ministry. Alongside the pop-up cafés and work to establish third places, activities include an artists' workshop for six to eleven year olds; a group for tots and parents called Messy Play; a mobile youth club; an English as a Second Language (ESL) class; a knitting group run by a local resident; a sewing club; and a cycling club for women that includes instructions on safe bicycling. During school breaks and the summer, the Engine Room also hosts cooking classes and activities geared toward youth and families with children such as kayaking, paintball, horse riding, or soccer.

The work of the Engine Room is complemented by a new church plant at Hale Village Estate called St. Francis Church. A new priest missioner, Andrew Williams, has been called, and he works with Andrew and Martina. The developers for Hale Village worked with the Diocese of London to create a church space in one of the newer buildings, which will be at the center of the entire development once it is finished—for now it is on the north edge. The new church opened in 2017, the first new church structure dedicated in London in almost forty years. It features flexible space, including a moveable altar and a walk-in baptismal font under a removable section of flooring. When not being used as a church or chapel, it can serve as community meeting space. After starting from nothing, St. Francis Church at the Engine Room today has a worship attendance from the mid-forties to low fifties each Sunday.

They have been deliberate to graft community organizing and engagement into the new church structure from the beginning: St. Francis not only has flexible space for worship services but also continues the work of the Engine Room, featuring a community center, a preschool, and a café. Plans are in place for a learning workshop for job skills, ESL classes, and other needed subjects.

As the church has come together, Andrew Kwapong shared a key learning point. On the one hand, he said, it was important for the church to begin its work on the Hale Village estate early, to be a part of the emerging community, to know the place and its people from the beginning, and to be a visible, listening presence at the Ferry Lane Estate. The church has been proactive there, rather than waiting for a group of people to request for them to be a part of the area. On the other hand, by starting out with a community center, by working with and listening to the community, the church planters have been able to discern the needs of the people. Rather than swooping in with a ready-made church or an imported form of mission that might have worked in Liverpool or New York, the church has proactively listened, been present, and journeyed with the people there, as well as sharing the good news of Jesus and planting a church.

This kind of genuine and compassionate engagement takes time to build trust and relationships. It is not easy or straightforward. But this work is important, never more so than when a community is in crisis.

In August 2011, police shot and killed a 29-year-old man in the road between the Hale Village and Ferry Lane Estate. In the subsequent days, rioting and looting roiled the nation. Although Hale Village is a pristine new housing development, the greater borough of Tottenham has one of the highest unemployment rates in the United Kingdom and is known to some as an area of gang activity and crime. A previous riot in 1985 left an uneasy tension between residents and police.

The area churches faced a significant test to this community approach: Would they shrink back in troubling times or would they be present with the people? Thankfully, the churches chose to walk with the people, being present both in the highs and the lows of life.

Several days after the riots began in Tottenham, they spread to neighboring Hackney. Rob Wickham, at the time rector of St. John at Hackney, remembers that night.

"You get a sixth sense almost. The day of the Tottenham riots, I told my wife they're going to break out in Hackney. Two days later, the deputy head and the head teacher of my secondary school phoned me up and said you need to know that Blackberry Messenger is going mad at the moment for people to come to Hackney to be difficult. 'I suggest you go home' is what they said. So of course I put on my cassock and went out and stood in the middle of it all. I saw the first brick being thrown. The only way I can describe it is that civil society just sort of moved out. Everyone packed up shop and disappeared, which left a huge void."[86] This allowed those who intended on causing trouble to move in without any resistance.

Rob not only went out on the streets to be with the people of the community, he called the local bishop in as well. The two of them were present, often standing between the police and the rioters. "The conversations we had were just extraordinary."

And at points, it was surreal. An elderly woman fell and broke her hip. Rob and the bishop talked with the rioters, explaining that they were trying to protect this woman and get her to safety. He explained that "it was like in Revelation, where there was a half hour of silence—just like that, everything stopped, for about ten or fifteen minutes. Space was made for an ambulance to come in to take her off. And as soon as they were gone, petrol bombs started going again."

Just as important as Rob's presence during the riots was the work he had done beforehand to build trust. Two years earlier, Rob officiated the funeral for a promising young soccer player tragically killed in a knife attack. The funeral gave him a chance to get to know the people in the broader community. When the riots came to Hackney, Rob knew many of the people on the street: police, bystanders, and rioters.

Even more important than his presence on the street that night was the church's response the next day. A clean-up operation was organized using Twitter. Around 2,000 people showed up on the town hall steps with buckets and brooms and mops, ready to go. Rob stood up and addressed the crowd, encouraging them to go to Clarence Road where the bulk of the destruction occurred. He had the volunteers gather in a big circle, and they had two minutes of silence. Rob invited those who were people of prayer to pray for the rioters, for the residents, and for the businesses. And then they got busy cleaning.

The next day, he invited people to a prayer vigil on the steps of the church. The bishop came to speak as did the leader of the borough council. Also invited to speak was a group of young people who had been working in Hackney as a part of CitySafe, a community-led campaign of Citizens UK to improve street safety by forming relationships among young people, businesses, and police. Rob explained that it was especially important to include these young people because so many people were blaming the rioting on "feral youth." About 200 people came out to light candles and pray for healing.

Two other incidents were pivotal. First, a convenience store owned and operated for eleven years by local resident Siva Kandiah was ransacked and burned. Although the building was covered by insurance, all his savings had been invested in stock, which was not covered. Rob and a team of local people created a "save the shop" fund with appeals on the Internet and television; over the next month, they managed to raise over £30,000 to help Siva restock his shop. Second, Rob worked with the manager of the local branch of Marks & Spencer, a British department store chain, to sponsor afternoon tea for 400 people. A week after the streets had been choked with violence, the streets were again closed—but this time with tables and chairs, tea and cakes, open-air music, hula hoops, and sidewalk chalk—and hundreds of people reclaimed their streets for their community.

These experiences offer dramatic but critical examples of what can happen when a church is truly engaged with the surrounding community. Building relationships is fundamental—and best done long before a moment of crisis. Church-led community organizing creates places for relationships to grow, working for the safety of the streets and neighborhoods and giving voice to those who are too often unnoticed or dismissed. In all these situations, the heart of the work is generous listening and relationship building.

Chapter 10
Learning from London

By way of conclusion, I offer several core convictions that I have formed through this project. I hope these spur some further thought, prayer, and action for you, in whatever setting you find yourself. In short, here is what I have learned from London:

First, **start with what God has already given you, not what you think you don't have.** It can be easy to look at one church or another and say, "Well, if we had that we'd be flourishing too." But the key here is that God has already given you all kinds of gifts that are sufficient for what God is calling you to. What gifts has God given you? What is God calling you to? Don't be distracted by or feel inferior to (or better than!) others who have different gifts; God has likely called them to do different things than you.

Never stop learning. While Holy Trinity Brompton is guided by some clear principles and core values, they are not so locked in to one method, one way of doing things, one possible outcome, that they cease listening and learning. They have modified Alpha over the years. They have embraced other, more sacramental forms of church services through their work with St. Augustine's. They have adapted and changed their model of church planting over the last couple of decades. They were willing to work with (and under) their bishop when other churches struck out on their own, I have become convinced that one of their overriding commitments is to remain faithful to God and God's call, to "play their part in the evangelization of the nation, the revitalization of the church, and the transformation of society," as their tagline reads. As they live this out, their ministry far transcends "keeping the show going" or "doing it like we've always done it." Life at HTB seems like one of ongoing incremental change—and sometimes rather more than incremental.

That's not to say that HTB has gotten everything right or is beyond criticism. (They wouldn't say so themselves.) Nor is it to say that learning from HTB means imitating them in all they've done. But one of my core convictions that I take away from my time with churches in London is this: **Never think you know in advance who you can learn from.** We might disagree with a brother or sister in Christ on a substantial matter. But too often, at least in the parts of the American church that I know, this would result in never being in conversation or relationship with that other. We end up being siloed off from each other and parochial in our isolation.

God gives freely; we should too. Give away your best. Especially if we're feeling anxious or fearful it can be tempting to try to grasp tightly to whatever we've got. What I've heard consistently in London, with church planting especially, is to "give away your best." When considering a new church plant, a new graft, a new group, or a new program, give away your best, and trust God to provide more to give away. It's critical to communicate this approach to people clearly and often so that everyone is on board and understands the strategy.

Related to this is: **Don't be afraid to fail**. It can be easy to want to avoid failing more than trying for success. But if you consider a failure as an important opportunity to learn—and if you're able to keep the personal and emotional stakes of trying something and it not working low enough—then you might instead find yourself trying something just to see if it will work, to see what you can learn. Not long ago, we heard about banks that were "too big to fail." I sometimes wonder if the key to a successful experiment in the church might be ensuring it is "small enough to fail"—or, course, flourish and succeed!

Whether with a church plant/restart, an existing congregation, or a fresh expression, **start small and work for growth!** HTB might be the single largest Church of England congregation in the world but they didn't start there. And you shouldn't confuse having the goal of "being large" with the goal of "growing." They're different. You might be large but stagnant; you might be small and growing.

Run Alpha. Or if you don't like Alpha, run another course—or make up your own. And keep in mind that Alpha is about hospitality and relationship as well as teaching. By all means put up a sign in front of the church or a billboard by the highway. But the vast majority of people come to Alpha because they are invited by someone they know. (The same is true of church in general.)

Learn the lesson of Alpha: **A new believer is a precious thing** and a valuable potential leader. This isn't because they are "fresh meat" and can take on the work you're tired of. It's because they actually remember what it was like—the kinds of questions and doubts they had—before embracing Christian faith, and they can sympathize with and connect with outsiders much more easily than can someone who's been a member since the 1970s and whose circles of acquaintances barely stretch beyond the core membership of church.

Anything worth doing is worth doing badly. You can't wait until you're perfect to start. It can be tempting to think that you need to get everything fixed in the congregation before you try any kind of outreach or connection with the surrounding community. That's a rabbit hole that is rather dangerous to fall down. Now clearly there might be some things "on fire" in a given congregation that need addressing. But if you expect everything to be perfect before you do any evangelism or inviting of newcomers, then where will all the imperfect newcomers find their place? Also, since the congregation won't ever be perfect, you'll probably never get to inviting new, imperfect folks in the first place.

Related to this, a parishioner once said to me that he was "all for" outreach, but he was worried that it would be at the expense of "inreach," by which I think he meant pastoral care within the congregation. But I think it's a false dichotomy: A congregation that is energized by faith (instead of just trying to keep things going) will naturally want to do both and will see the two as mutually reinforcing rather than competing for scarce resources. The priest who visits someone at work for lunch or the small group Bible study who walks with a member in her grief or suffering is part of caring and witnessing. Why not do it intentionally as *both*? **Don't get caught up in either/or thinking.**

Be willing to plant churches and to encourage and support those who do. I ran into a diocese a few years ago that had last planted a new church in the 1950s. After forty years, that congregation closed. The operating assumption, therefore, was that church plants don't work, and they weren't going to try any more. (Never mind that there were numerous thriving recent church plants, many nondenominational, dotted throughout that region.)

This might be an extreme example, but the fact is that much of the Episcopal Church (with some welcome notable exceptions) has gotten out of the practice of planting churches. This is despite the fact that planting churches has been shown to be one of the most effective means of evangelism and church growth. Sometimes I think that we imagine that our congregations were simply formed when the earth's crust cooled, as much a feature of the landscape as a lake or mountain: They've just always been there. The truth is, every church was once planted, even the churches in Rome, Alexandria, Damascus, and Jerusalem. And in much of America, the population continues to grow and shift. If many of our congregations were planted in the middle nineteenth century, or the early twentieth century, or just after World War II, then it is likely that the population has grown substantially since then and often in areas far from where the population was centered in those earlier eras.

Be willing to think and work creatively to start new congregations, including Fresh Expressions of Church. Too often in America, we assume a church plant needs everything that an existing congregation needs: a building, a parking lot, paid full-time clergy, vestments, flower guild, a service register, and so forth. To plant a church you actually only need people with faith in the good news of God in Christ. They can meet in a living room, a community center, another church building, a pub or coffeehouse, wherever. They can be a new congregation of an existing church, meeting at a different day or time. The congregation may be lay led, bringing in clergy for eucharist from time to time. The possibilities are as wide as our imagination—and God's call and gifts.

There is nothing wrong with a building, a parking lot, paid full-time clergy, vestments, flower guild, a service register, and so forth, per se. But we often think of the church mostly in these terms. It is common to consider church something like (as church researcher Robert Warren puts it):

Church = building + priest + Sunday services.

But he suggests that this mental model is ripe for rethinking. One way to better reflect the church is a readjustment to the equation:

Church = community + faith + action.

Warren writes that "church is essentially a *community* of people drawn together by *faith* in and encounter with Jesus Christ as Lord, which leads them to take *action* in the whole of life, living by a different set of values from what would otherwise have been the case. This living will involve a wide range of 'actions' including both attitudes (such as listening or generosity) and actions (service, confrontation, or care)."[87]

This gets at what noted Fresh Expressions authority Michael Moynagh means when he talks about the "essence" of the church versus the "essentials" of the church. He says that the *essence* of the church is found in four interlocking relationships, centered on Jesus: "directly with God (through prayer, worship, and study), with the wider church, with the world, and within the fellowship" (i.e. a local, particular congregation). These relationships are the essence of what the church is and does and can be summarized as UP, IN, OUT, and OF. *Essential* to establishing, nurturing, and sustaining these relationships are practices such as preaching, the sacraments, and an ordered ministry.[88] It's like getting married; in the United States, you need a marriage license to get married—it's *essential*. But if anyone told you that the *essence* of being married was having a license, you'd be mystified.

Warren and Moynagh help us to think about just what we need for a congregation. Parking lots, flowers, vestments, service registers, even buildings are well down the list. Of those elements that are essential—preaching, sacraments, ordered ministry—the questions become: How are they serving the essence of the church where you are? How would they serve the essence of the church in a new congregation or church plant?

Don't become so enchanted with the tools that you lose sight of the task. I have an acquaintance who wanted to learn more about something known as "dinner church." I asked him who he was trying to reach with this interesting form of fresh expressions, and he seemed a bit confused. It was like he had gone to Home Depot and found a really fun tool and only later was going to look for something to do with it. But authentic fresh expressions start with relationships; whatever form the new Christian community takes follows from the people you're engaging. Warren and Moynagh help us to see this and remind us that even the tried-and-true tools that we've used before may need to be reconsidered in light of the task we've been given.

It's not all about you. I've met a few clergy and lay leaders who are very keen on Fresh Expressions of Church, but after talking with them for a while, I find their interest is because they themselves are dismayed at or bored with the inherited church as they know it. It's important that they recognize this and address this for themselves. But starting a fresh expression of church out of your own dissatisfaction—essentially, starting it for yourself—seems to cut off the important tasks of learning, listening, and serving that are crucial to fresh expressions.

If you are thinking about starting a fresh expression of church, be guided by questions at each stage: Who is in your world, outside of your congregation? What are they facing? How can you love and serve them well? What kind of opportunities are there to create community? What chance will you have to explore discipleship together? How will you see a new Christian community take shape? How will you do it again? Remember that a fresh expression of church, at least eventually, comprises *all* these stages. Undertake this with openness but also intentionality.

Don't get distracted by silly arguments. At times when I'm talking about growing churches or evangelism, someone will respond (perhaps with some snark) that they don't think we should be worried about "butts in pews," as if it's all about numbers or making a budget. But this always seems silly to me, an attitude motivated more by fear or defensiveness than anything. Let me put it this way: If someone were talking about working for social justice, how would it sound if someone piped up (with some knowing cynicism) that he didn't think we should be worried about "balming people's guilty consciences," as though we only did it to feel better about ourselves. There are mixed motivations for everything we do, that's no secret, and that's true for evangelism *and* social justice. But even with mixed motivations, the two really go hand in hand. I like the way that Bishop Paul Bayes, of the Diocese of Liverpool, puts it: "We are asking God for a bigger church so we can make a bigger difference—more people knowing Jesus, more justice in the world."[89] I've seen a similar both/and attitude among most churches in London.

A growing church doesn't necessarily mean a single massive congregation. Growth doesn't have to be about larger and larger crowds and progressively larger buildings. If you embrace growth along with an attitude of giving away your best, then perhaps your growing congregation will also train, gift, and empower its members to go and start something new somewhere else—maybe becoming a church that plants churches like St. Paul's, Shadwell. Or you may find that you have a congregation that fills its space on a Sunday (there's not much room for growth) or functions in such a way that growth would be difficult. Instead of trying to sled uphill, this can be an opportunity for the congregation to duplicate itself (instead of growing larger) or else plant another congregation altogether. This is the situation that St. Peter's, Bethnal Green, found itself in, so they started a Sunday evening service for younger adults that later became a part of a separate church plant.

Be yourself. But also work to be a better self, growing in how you reflect the love of God for the world. Many churches are strongly attached to their forms of expression and worship: I have Anglo-Catholic friends who would break out in hives at the mere suggestion that they might put in some screens and have a praise band. I have evangelical friends who would feel sick to their stomachs if I suggested they might have a chanted high mass with incense. This might be overstating the point, but we can become very defensive when there is the possibility that we will be asked to give up what we hold as precious and life-giving. For my part, I don't think there is much reason to forsake one style for another. The important thing is to work to ensure that whatever form of church you inhabit is serving the gospel of Christ and loving and serving the world in his name. So, be yourself, but don't be self-satisfied.

If you're a clergyperson, remember that you share this work with the rest of the congregation. It's not your job to do it all: Share your authority and your learning.

If you're a layperson, remember that this work is yours, by virtue of being baptized. Don't expect (or allow) your priest to do it all. Accept and lean into your role as a disciple of Christ and a missionary in whatever culture you find yourself.

Remember: We are called to be cross-cultural missionaries, bearing witness to Christ. Don't expect a visitor, newcomer, or someone unaffiliated with the church to be the cross-cultural missionary, entering in on his or her own and leaving the person to make sense of it all. There are many ways to bear witness: Alpha and similar courses are one. Changing the forms of music, the language we use, and the aesthetic we embrace is another. Yet another is to change none of that but to do it all with excellence and focus on intentionally inviting people in and being engaged with them to help them along over time. The liturgy can be mysterious—especially if its leader and participants are reluctant to interact with someone new—and the language for someone unfamiliar with the church might be opaque. It might even be that a number of longtime members haven't the foggiest notion what is going on and steer clear of newcomers out of defensiveness. But the liturgy can also be mysterious because it is about the depths of God and God's ways with the world and our life in Christ. Make sure your worship embraces the right kind of mystery! The key is being intentional in invitation and in translation.

Be gentle but clear about your faith. Particularly in London, most churches assume they need to speak for themselves and can't assume that everyone knows about or understands the basics of the Christian faith.

In America for some time we've been able to skate, assuming that most everyone knows what Christianity is about, and if they decide that's what they want, they'll come to church, maybe even our church. The task of making an appeal, bearing witness, translating the faith to those outside of the church often goes undone or is carried out with a heavy hand.

We can all think of examples of churches that have been manipulative or inauthentic or inappropriate in some other way, especially with helping the vulnerable. Too often, though,

I've run into churches that, because of these bad examples, are reluctant to say or do anything from their faith. One congregation I know has a huge feeding ministry for its town at the end of the month. It attracts several hundred people, the vast majority of whom are not connected with this church or any congregation. I asked them about the meal, and they volunteered that they do not do anything "religious" in connection with it: They don't pray before the meal, don't invite anybody for anything else, don't talk about the church's life, don't do anything related to the faith. Originally they had decided not to do anything faith-related because they didn't want to seem too pushy. I understand not wanting to be pushy or not wanting to be conditional in your care (I'll feed you if you come to church). But when you are a congregation serving a meal to people in the basement of a church building as part of the church's ministry, the cat's already out of the bag. From my perspective, this reluctance to bear witness is an overreaction to others' cynical or manipulative service. Being completely silent risks sending—or reinforcing—the message that "we're not really interested in sharing something very good with you. You're not our kind of people. You wouldn't fit in here. We're happy to feed the hungry, but we don't really want to get to know you as equals." Far better to embrace the vulnerability of gently bearing witness, getting to know people, risking getting to know them as sisters, brothers, maybe friends, and maybe even needing to make some adjustments in the service for those who are new to the faith or the Anglican tradition but who have found someone wonderful in Jesus Christ.

Don't expect others to do the work of sharing the gospel. If others have done it badly, the remedy is not to refuse to do it but to do it better.

Honor the past; navigate change in the present; build for the future. Bishop Ric Thorpe shared this with me early on in my investigations, and it has seemed important for understanding both how church plants and in-grafts have functioned as well as how all the leadership of the diocese work at their best—and how we may too. This is not a matter of clearing away all the valuable heritage for "the new." We are called to positive change to remain faithful and pass on the faith. And we take the long view, not just trying to get through the week, or the programming year, or to retirement. Instead we ask: "How will we have a thriving church to turn over to the next generation, and how will that generation be here to receive it as something good?"

Finally, remember that **we don't undertake this work for ourselves.** We are not building empires for ourselves, not trying to make our church budgets, not trying to hold on to the way we've always done things, or even trying to change for the sake of change. We are following God's call to be God's ambassadors, sharing the good news of reconciliation and new life in Jesus Christ, for the life and health of the world. God draws us in to God's work in the world, entrusts us with this ministry, and accompanies us in this work. What an awesome and humbling task. May God empower us to do it.

Acknowledgments

As I look back over the years I've put into this work, I realize that I owe many people a debt of gratitude for their time and energy in helping this book come to completion.

Chief among these are the faithful servants of the servants of Christ, working in the church in London. These include Richard Chartres, the longtime bishop of London who encouraged the work in a number of ways; likewise Stephen Cottrell, bishop of Chelmsford, was enthusiastic to hear of the project and generous with his time.

As well, my gratitude extends to a number of people who, since I first met them have become bishops in the church, including Ric Thorpe of St. Paul's, Shadwell, now bishop of Islington; Rachel Treweek, archdeacon of Hackney and now bishop of Gloucester; Rob Wickham of St. John at Hackney, now bishop of Edmonton; and Graham Tomlin of St. Mellitus College, now bishop of Kensington. Whether this is an identifiable effect of spending time with me is, of course, highly doubtful!

Many people in and around the Diocese of London gave time and energy to help me understand their ministry and the growth in the diocese. These include Nick Mercer, sometime vicar general for the Diocese of London; James Walters, of the London School of Economics, both of whom were very helpful at the genesis of this project. Alongside these, I am particularly grateful for the generosity of Pete Broadbent, bishop of Willesden; Luke Miller, archdeacon of Hampstead, now archdeacon of London; Mark Elsdon-Dew of Holy Trinity, Brompton; Bonnie Yule-Kuehne, Toby Flint, Dave Mathews of Alpha; Tim Thorlby and Angus Ritchie of the Centre for Theology & Community; John Wood, formerly of St. Ann's, Tottenham; Adam Boyce and the team at London City Mission; Simon Morris of St. Mary's, Tottenham; Nicholas Wheeler of Holy Trinity, Sloane Square; Jane Hodges of the parish of All Saints, Poplar; Will Leaf, formerly of St. Paul's, Hammersmith, now at St. Mark's, Kensal Rise; Frances Shoesmith and Donna Gwilliams of St. Luke's in the High Street; Will Cookson and Sue Bosley of Springfield Church; H Miller of the Centre for Church Planting & Growth; Annie McTighe of Church E 20 and the Olympic Village pioneer ministry; Ed Dix and Tom Pyke on the Isle of Dogs; Adam Atkinson of St. Peter's, Bethnal Green; Niall Weir of St. Paul's, West Hackney; Sam Wells of St. Martin-in-the-Fields; Lucy Winkett of St. James', Piccadilly; Stephen Mason of St. John's, Hyde Park; Andrew Kwapong of the Engine Room, and Andrew Williams of St. Francis Church, Hale Village; Annie Kirke, Mark Bishop, and Phil Hoyle working with Missional Communities; and Adrian Chatfield and Michael Moynagh, working in Fresh Expressions.

I am grateful for all of the students who have gone on my Learning from London class, asking questions and making observations, and helping my own learning. I am especially thankful for those who took the time to read early versions of this manuscript and make remarks and suggestions.

Essential to my being able to do this work has been the generous funding that I received from The Episcopal Evangelism Society and several Conant Grants from The Episcopal Church.

Richelle Thompson and Scott Gunn of Forward Movement shared their enthusiasm for this project from the beginning and even provided me with energy when it seemed to flag; I'm grateful for their encouragement. Jana Riess helped my prose style immensely, as I transitioned from writing for scholars to writing for a much wider audience.

Finally, my researching the church in London has meant actually being in London, buying people coffee, listening to stories, and getting to know the churches there firsthand. This has also meant that I have often had to be five time zones away from my family, including my wife, Kristen, and my two daughters, Alexandra and Samantha. Every time I am in London, I am filled with excitement for what God is doing in the church there and for what we can learn for ourselves; I am likewise filled with a wistful longing to be with those I love most, missing them dearly. They, too, have been kind, generous, and sacrificial in helping this project come to fruition, and it is to my two daughters, Alex and Sam, that I dedicate this book.

Additional Reading

Alpha and Evangelism

Stephen Cottrell, *From the Abundance of the Heart: Catholic Evangelism for All Christians.* London: Darton, Longman & Tod. 2006.

Nicky Gumbel, *Telling Others: How to Run the Alpha Course.* London: Alpha International. 2011.

Mark Ireland and Mike Booker, *Making New Disciples: Exploring the Paradoxes of Evangelism.* London: SPCK. 2017.

Fresh Expressions of Church

Archbishop's Council on Mission and Public Affairs, *Mission-Shaped Church: Church Planting and Fresh Expressions in a Changing Context.* London: Church House. 2004.

Sally Gaze, *Mission-shaped and Rural: Growing Churches in the Countryside.* Norwich: Hymns Ancient & Modern. 2011.

David Goodhew, Andrew Roberts, Michael Volland, *Fresh! An Introduction to Fresh Expressions of Church and Pioneer Ministry.* London: SCM Press. 2012.

Michael Moynagh, *Being Church, Doing Life: Creating Gospel Communities Where Life Happens*. Oxford: Monarch Books. 2014.

Michael Moynagh, *Church in Life: Innovation, Mission and Ecclesiology*. London: SCM Press. 2017.

Church Planting

Jonny Baker and Cathy Ross, eds., *The Pioneer Gift: Explorations in Mission*. Norwich: Canterbury Press. 2014.

Christopher B. James, *Church Planting in Post-Christian Soil: Theology and Practice*. Oxford: Oxford University Press. 2018.

Ed Stetzer and Daniel Im, *Planting Missional Churches: Your Guide to Starting Churches that Multiply*. 2d ed. Nashville: B&H Academic. 2016.

Healthy, Growing Churches

Paul Bayes and Tim Sledge eds., *Mission-Shaped Parish: Traditional Church in a Changing World*. London: Church House Publishing. 2010.

Mike Chew and Mark Ireland, *How to Do Mission Action Planning: A Vision-Centred Approach*. London: SPCK. 2009.

Bob Jackson, *The Road to Growth: Towards a Thriving Church*. London: Church House Publishing. 2005.

Timothy Keller, *Center Church: Doing Balanced, Gospel-Centered Ministry in Your City*. Grand Rapids, MI: Zondervan. 2012.

George Lings, *Reproducing Churches*. Abingdon, UK: Bible Reading Fellowship. 2017.

Paul Sparks, Tim Soerens, and Dwight J. Friesen, *The New Parish: How Neighborhood Churches are Transforming Mission, Discipleship, and Community.* Downers Grove, IL: IVP Books. 2014.

Robert Warren, *The Healthy Churches' Handbook: A Process for Revitalizing Your Church.* London: Church House Publishing. 2004.

Robert Warren, *Developing Healthy Churches: Returning to the Heart of Mission and Ministry.* London: Church House Publishing. 2012.

Theological Resources

David Goodhew, ed., *Church Growth in Britain: 1980 to the Present.* Ashgate Contemporary Ecclesiology Series. Burlington, VT: Ashgate. 2012.

David Goodhew, ed., *Towards a Theology of Church Growth.* Ashgate Contemporary Ecclesiology Series. Burlington, VT: Ashgate. 2015.

Ann Morisy, *Journeying Out: A New Approach to Christian Mission.* New York: Continuum. 2006.

Andrew Rumsey, *Parish: An Anglican Theology of Place.* London: SCM Press. 2017.

Graham Tomlin, *The Provocative Church.* 4th ed. Cincinnati, OH: Forward Movement. 2015.

Samuel Wells, *A Nazareth Manifesto: Being With God.* Malden, MA: Wiley Press. 2015.

Endnotes

[1] What in previous times we've called "churchmanship"

[2] http://sps.church/ retrieved January 4, 2018

[3] The Money Course is a part of Crosslight Advice, which is an independent charity that works to eliminate "poverty and hardship caused by the burden of unmanageable debt and lack of financial capability." (from the Crosslight website, retrieved January 4, 2018.) Crosslight is able to not only provide information about budgeting and money management, but within the United Kingdom's charitable aid system, it is also able to mediate between someone in debt and creditors or others threatening legal action.

[4] See, for example, Daniel Im, "Multiplication is Impossible Without Intentionality" http://www.christianitytoday.com/edstetzer/2015/november/multiplication-is-impossible-without-intentionality.html accessed January 6, 2016

[5] See, for example, Ed Stetzer, "New Research: Survey Says Spiritual Maturity Comes through Intentionality" http://www.christianitytoday.com/edstetzer/2014/february/new-research-survey-says-spiritual-maturity-comes-through-i.html accessed January 6, 2016

[6] Robert Warren, *The Healthy Churches' Handbook*. London: Church House Publishing. 2004. p. 44

[7] https://extranet.generalconvention.org/staff/files/download/22940 accessed August 30, 2018

[8] The present day Diocese of London covers only a fraction of the city of London, roughly 40 percent of greater London, including boroughs near the center of the city and more suburban areas, commonly

known as "inner" and "outer" boroughs respectively. The Diocese of Southwark takes in nearly all of the city of London south of the Thames River, apart from two boroughs in the east and a single parish in the west. North of the Thames, five boroughs of eastern London are included in the Diocese of Chelmsford, which also takes in the county of Essex. Finally, part of the borough of Barnet, in the northern end of London, is included in the Diocese of St. Alban's.

[9] http://www.brin.ac.uk/london-churchgoing-and-other-news/ and https://www.pewforum.org/religious-landscape-study/attendance-at-religious-services/ from their 2014 survey accessed May 23, 2019

[10] From 2002-2012 they grew by 16 percent in terms of ASA (52,800 in 2002 (from Diocese of London's "Another Capital Idea" document) to 61,300 in 2012 (from Church of England "Statistics for Mission" 2012), for a growth of around 8,500 people, around 16 percent.

[11] Numbers for 2017 were available for the Episcopal Church but not the Church of England as of this writing.

[12] https://www.london.anglican.org/mission/capital-vision-2020/cv2020-media/, "Reasons to Celebrate" postcard, accessed September 5, 2018

[13] See, for example, http://www.episcopalcafe.com/lead/Domestic%20%20FAST%20FACTS%202003-2007.pdf or https://www.episcopalchurch.org/files/domestic_fast_facts_trends_2007-2011.pdf or https://extranet.generalconvention.org/staff/files/download/22938.

[14] Diocese of London, "A Capital Idea." 2003. p. 38

[15] "A Capital Idea," p. 48

[16] Diocese of London, "Another Capital Idea," 2012. p. 77

[17] "Another Capital Idea," p. 73

[18] "A Capital Idea," p. 7

[19] "A Capital Idea," p. 7, 8

[20] This can be compared with other dioceses in growing areas. For example, the City of New York grew by an estimated 5.5% between 2010 and 2017; in that same time span, Average Sunday Attendance in the Diocese of New York (which comprises a sizeable portion of the

city and several suburban counties) plunged by around 14 percent. Clearly a growing population does not translate instantly to a growing church.

[21] Madeleine Davies, "Clergy flock to fill posts in 'wealthy' south-east," *Church Times*, 7 Feb 2014, http://www.churchtimes.co.uk/articles/2014/7-february/news/uk/clergy-flock-to-fill-posts-in-%E2%80%98wealthy%E2%80%99-south-east

[22] https://crtrust.org/church-plants

[23] "Another Capital Idea," p. 35, 36

[24] "A Capital Idea," p. 13

[25] Richard Chartres, "New Fire in London", Lambeth Lecture delivered September 30, 2015. (Available at: http://www.london.anglican.org/articles/new-fire-in-london-lambeth-lecture/)

[26] Catherine Ellerby, "Church Growth in an Urban Parish," *Resourcing Mission Bulletin*, March 2014. p. 12, 13

[27] Since I first became acquainted with St. John at Hackney, Rob Wickham has become area bishop of Edmonton in London (2015). It is unclear whether this particular MAP remains active in this congregation.

[28] SMART goals summary from the Diocese of London website: http://www.london.anglican.org/kb/mission-action-planning/ accessed January 4, 2016

[29] "New Fire in London"

[30] The four Capital Investments are: 1) Recruit and train 2012 ambassadors for Jesus Christ under the age of 35 by 2012; 2) Increase provision in Church of England secondary schools in the diocese by 2012 places by 2012; 3) Raise £2,012,000 for development in Africa by 2012; and 4) Raise £2,012,000 to support the Home Mission Fund by 2012. (from the *London Challenge 2012* brochure.)

[31] http://www.london.anglican.org/about/london-challenge/ retrieved on January 4, 2016

[32] Debbie Clinton and staff of the Strategy Development Unity, "Capital Vision 2020," *Resourcing Mission Bulletin*, October 2013, p.1

[33] http://www.london.anglican.org/mission/capital-vision-2020/ accessed on January 4, 2016

[34] Coined by Jim Collins and Jerry Porras in their 1994 book *Built to Last: Successful Habits of Visionary Companies*.

[35] Bishop Chartres jokes that he initially wanted the goal to be 144,000 (twice as many as members in the diocese) but staff members were worried it would sound too much like the Jehovah's Witnesses, who believe this represents the total number of those who will go to heaven!

[36] A website dedicated to the goal explains more, saying that it is about encouraging and equipping followers of Jesus Christ to "live and work to his praise and glory in daily life." http://www.ambassadors2020.org/ accessed October 31, 2016

[37] From "New Fire in London"

[38] As related to me by Mark Elsdon-Dew

[39] From interview with Mark Elsdon-Dew

[40] In fact, much of the format can change depending on needs and resources: For example, an Alpha group running in the mornings for parents with toddlers may not have a meal involved but would certainly include skilled child care as an expression of love and care for those taking the course.

[41] https://static1.squarespace.com/static/56d056fb40261db4d8f2f5af/t/56fbaf3b40261dc6fac3db35/1459334982116/Alpha_Basics.pdf

[42] Although there was a time early on when the Alpha materials were not copyrighted, this resulted in some churches taking the materials and adapting them in ways that HTB did not think were for the best.

[43] *Diocese of London Church Planting* policy paper, found on http://bishopofwillesden.blogspot.com/2015/04/church-planting.html, accessed November 11, 2016

[44] Ray Oldenburg, *The Great Good Place*. New York: Marlowe & Co., 1999.

[45] More forms are set out here: http://www.missionalcommunities.london/about/fiveways

[46] C. Peter Wagner, *Strategies for Church Growth*. Glendale, CA: Regal. 1987. p. 168

[47] There is a story, possibly apocryphal, told about the initial meeting of the leadership of HTB with the bishop of London to discuss starting church planting. It is said that the bishop asked what HTB would do if he didn't give them permission. They said that they might do it anyway, just outside of the structures of the Church of England. Taking a moment to consider the situation, the bishop's eyes came to rest on a painting hanging on his wall: a portrait of John Wesley. Realizing with a start the historical precedent—and the centuries of walking apart that the Church of England and the Methodists have experienced—the bishop decided that the best course of action would be to permit and cooperate with these church plants and see what kinds of fruit would come from continuing this relationship instead of letting it be severed.

[48] p. 40

[49] https://www.htb.org/shelter

[50] CGRP, *Church Planting*, p. 19

[51] I spoke with Ric in the summer of 2014, when he was rector of St. Paul's and Bishop of London's Adviser for Church Planting; in September 2015, he became the bishop of Islington, a revival of an old bishopric, now focused on being a "bishop for church plants" with responsibilities in London as well as the Church of England as a whole.

[52] St Paul's is clear that the ministry of the kids' and caregivers' group is chiefly to the caregivers: giving (mostly) moms a chance to get out, to connect with other adults, to enjoy a cup of coffee or tea and some cake, and to connect with the church in a nonthreatening and low-key way, coming in over the threshold and being blessed by what happens there.

[53] CGRP, *Church Planting*, p. 20

[54] See "'Tottenham doesn't need hope bringing to it by some Oxbridge geek'–Queen's Birthday Honours Vicar" in *Tottenham Journal*, June 20, 2014, by Stephen Moore. http://www.tottenhamjournal.co.uk/news/queen_s_birthday_honours_vicar_john_wood_tottenham_doesn_t_

need_hope_oxbridge_geek_st_ann_s_church_1_3650119 accessed November 16, 2016

[55] It is all the more striking—and surprising—then that Sarah Mullally was appointed bishop of London in December 2017, succeeding Bishop Richard Chartres, who retired earlier that year.

[56] Chartres, "New Fire in London" 2015

[57] Tim Thorlby, "A Time to Sow", p. 76. http://www.theology-centre.org.uk/wp-content/uploads/2013/04/CTC-Research-Report-9-A-Time-To-Sow-2017online.pdf accessed January 4, 2018

[58] Thorlby, "A Time to Sow", p. 77, 78

[59] Thorlby, "A Time to Sow", p. 78

[60] Sadly, Betjeman's approval is not enough in itself to save a church: he worshiped at a similarly grand Arts and Crafts style church, St. Saviour's Aberdeen Park, which he immortalized in verse. While it remains as a grade-I listed building, it now houses an art gallery and not a church.

[61] "New Fire in London"

[62] "London Stories: At the Heart of the Community," Diocese of London report on The London Challenge 2012, p. 11

[63] https://www.theguardian.com/commentisfree/belief/2011/aug/10/tottenham-riots-church

[64] I have not encountered Christingle outside of Britain. It is a simple service of prayers, readings, hymns or carols, and often a collection in support of the work of a charity for children. The Christingle—meaning "Christ light"—is an orange (symbolizing the world), wrapped in a red ribbon (symbolizing the love of God), with dried fruits or candy on toothpicks stuck into the orange, holding on the red ribbon. A candle is placed into the top of the orange: This represents the light of Christ bringing hope to people in a darkened world. The candle is lit during the service. The services are accessible to everyone, even if they have no particular church background. In America (or whatever your context) you could adapt such a service or create your own with similar purposes.

[65] See the next chapter for more on Messy Church.

[66] Our Lady of Walsingham is a popular English Marian shrine located east of England.

[67] The diocese has even made available an "Open Churches Toolkit," available online: http://www.london.anglican.org/support/buildings-and-property/open-churches-toolkit/ accessed January 7, 2016

[68] For more information, visit http://bethlehem-unwrapped.org/ accessed January 7, 2016

[69] http://www.london.anglican.org/articles/award-for-west-hackney-recreation-ground/ accessed January 7, 2016

[70] http://www.london.anglican.org/articles/pause-discover-pray-opening-up-st-marys-islington/ accessed January 7, 2016

[71] http://www.london.anglican.org/articles/st-marys-islington-increases-attendance-as-it-keeps-its-doors-open-to-the-community/ accessed January 7, 2016

[72] http://www.london.anglican.org/articles/pause-discover-pray-opening-up-st-marys-islington/ accessed January 7, 2016

[73] In the UK this is rather different than what in the US is sometimes termed "debt counseling." Crosslight and similar services (some of which are for-profit) have a legal standing to help their clients negotiate taxes, rents, fees and so forth, and to enter into payment arrangements.

[74] The phrase Fresh Expressions of Church originated with the Church of England report *Mission-Shaped Church: Church Planting and Fresh Expressions in a Changing Context*. London: Church House Publishing. 2004. The term has taken off in multiple denomination in the UK and is found in the US and elsewhere too.

[75] http://aoc2013.brix.fatbeehive.com/articles.php/2044/making-the-mixed-economy-work, accessed April 9, 2019

[76] Generally, the movement is known as Fresh Expressions of Church (with capitals), but individual groups are known as fresh expressions (no caps).

[77] I'm grateful to Michael Moynagh for these specific approaches.

[78] http://community.sharetheguide.org/guide/develop/journey accessed October 18, 2017

[79] https://www.freshexpressions.org.uk/stories/stlukesinthehighstreet/aug13

[80] St Luke's in the High Street is a part of the parish of Walthamstow, which also includes St. Mary's and St. Gabriel's. St. Luke's is a part of this team, although they no longer have a full-time ordained leader.

[81] Wolfgang Simson, *The House Church Book*. Tyndale House. 2009. p. 31

[82] A "person of peace" is an idea rooted in the Gospel of Luke, chapter ten. Jesus sent out 72 people to prepare the way for Jesus to come. In verses 5-7, Jesus says that if you enter a house and a person who "shares in peace" is there, then stay, eating and drinking whatever they provide, and not moving around. In contemporary usage, this is taken to be someone who is open to Christ (not necessarily a believer) and who is known in and likely respected by the community, someone who is credible and connected.

[83] https://www.cofepioneer.org/essential/ accessed December 15, 2017

[84] Other stories of pioneer ministers across the Church of England (not just London) may be found at https://www.cofepioneer.org/stories/ accessed December 15, 2017

[85] Oldenburg, *The Great Good Place*. 1999

[86] Related in conversation

[87] Robert Warren. *The Healthy Churches' Handbook*. London: Church House Publishing. 2004. p. 85

[88] Michael Moynagh, *Church in Life: Innovation, Mission, and Ecclesiology.* SCM Press, 2017. p. 241, 245

[89] http://www.liverpool.anglican.org/BiggerChurchBiggerDifference, retrieved April 23, 2019.

About the Author

Jason A. Fout has taught at Bexley Seabury Seminary Federation (and before that, Bexley Hall) since 2009, as associate professor of Anglican theology. Originally from Chicago, he studied at the University of Illinois at Chicago, Seabury Western Theological Seminary, and The University of Cambridge. He now resides in the Columbus, Ohio, area, dividing his teaching between Chicago and London. In London, he teaches a course called "Learning from London," a weeklong dive into the mission and ministry there, building on the foundation laid by this book. Although he does not serve a congregation, he is passionate about helping to stimulate conversation among clergy and lay leaders about creative, faithful ministry.

It has often been remarked that England and the United States are two nations separated by a common language. Jason often finds himself in the situation of translating the Church of England (in which he was licensed to serve for four years) to the Episcopal Church (in which he has been a priest since 2001), and vice versa. We are, it seems, two churches separated by a common tradition.

About Forward Movement

Forward Movement is committed to inspiring disciples and empowering evangelists. Our ministry is lived out by creating resources such as books, small-group studies, apps, and conferences.

Our daily devotional, *Forward Day by Day*, is also available in Spanish (*Adelante Día a Día*) and Braille, online, as a podcast, and as an app for smartphones or tablets. It is mailed to more than fifty countries, and we donate nearly 30,000 copies each quarter to prisons, hospitals, and nursing homes.

We actively seek partners across the church and look for ways to provide resources that inspire and challenge. A ministry of the Episcopal Church for over eighty years, Forward Movement is a nonprofit organization funded by sales of resources and by gifts from generous donors.

To learn more about Forward Movement and our resources, visit www.ForwardMovement.org. We are delighted to be doing this work and invite your prayers and support.